For Margaret from Bill,
Editor-in-Chief and
author of Part III

16 July 1986

**HMSO**

1786-1986

This HMSO Bicentenary emblem
incorporates the Royal Arms first used on official printing during
the reign of George III when Her Majesty's Stationery Office
was established.

# HER MAJESTY'S STATIONERY OFFICE

The story of the first 200 years
1786 – 1986

Hugh Barty-King

ISBN 0 11 701304 8

Produced for Her Majesty's Stationery Office by:
MC Typeset, Chatham (typesetting)
East Anglian Engraving Co. Ltd., Norwich (reproduction)
APB Process Print Ltd., Bristol (printing)
Cedric Chivers Ltd., Bath (binding)

# Contents

# Acknowledgements

My thanks are due to Mr W.J. Sharp, Controller and Chief Executive, for giving me of his time to talk to me about various aspects of HMSO activity from 1980 onwards, and for his comments on the draft manuscript; to the two Directors-General, Mr A.A. Smith and Mr K.A. Allen, for their guidance and advice; and to Mr M.J.M. Salt who was my liaison with HMSO from the beginning of the project in April 1983 right through to its final stage. Mr D.C. Dashfield, who retired as a Director General in 1981 after spending the whole of his working life in HMSO (as did his father), was kind enough to review the text. The interest he acquired during the course of his career in the history of HMSO and his direct knowledge and experience made his suggestions and painstaking editing of very great value.

The late Mr W. Cox, Deputy Controller from 1953 to 1959, dug deep into the available archival material for the four memorandums which he wrote for internal use in 1961 and 1963, and his authoritative exposition of problems and events has been a useful source for the present work. I was also grateful for the comments of the late Mr C.G. Lloyd who read an early draft of the manuscript before his death in 1985, and to the many present and retired HMSO staff who assisted me in my investigations.

While there was a celebration of a hundred years of Vote Funding in 1924 there was no history; and there was neither celebration nor history for the centenary of the establishment of the Stationery Office in 1886. The full story has had to be told here for the first time. For the main documents on the foundation of the Stationery Office I went to the Public Record Office at Kew where my task was greatly eased by Mr D.C. Chalmers, Head of Search Department; and for documents covering the whole period to the HMSO Archive at Norwich.

I am grateful to Mr K. Morgan and Mr I. Church, Editor and Assistant Editor of the Commons Official Report (*Hansard*), Mr M.T. Ryle, Principal Clerk of the Table Office and Mr H.C. Foster, Deputy Deliverer of the Vote, who showed me around and talked to me about their work in the course of my visit to the House of Commons.

I also acknowledge the help given by Mr John Philips, Head of the Maps and Prints Department of the Greater London Record Office and History Library; Mr E. Jones, Company Secretary, Harrison & Sons; Mr D.S. Paravicini, Secretary, Mr A. Napier and Mr J. Maynard, The De La Rue Company; and Mr Robert H. Cole, The British Printing & Communications Corporation (Waterlows).

H.B-K
Ticehurst, August 1985

# List of illustrations

# Foreword

I commissioned Mr Barty-King to write this history of Her Majesty's Stationery Office to mark our Bicentenary year, 1986. The author has clearly brought out how considerably HMSO has changed over the years, both in size and business style.

Initially a tiny agency with as few as 17 staff (plus two horses and a cart) concerned primarily with replacing the existing random and corrupt system of purchasing Government stationery with honest and efficient methods, its very success led to considerable growth. In the course of the nineteenth century the Stationery Office expanded, with the support of HM Treasury, into printing for both Parliament and Government, and into publishing on a large scale. It is now the largest print buyer in the United Kingdom, one of the top British publishers, and has a large business which trades in office supplies. The natural and sturdy progression towards this situation was significantly quickened by the advent of the Great War, which led the Stationery Office to assume major responsibilities in the field for assisting the British Army in France and subsequently to service the Versailles Peace Conference. As always, the Office responded to operational challenges and adapted to meet them over the years.

The Second World War and its aftermath again led to major growth as the Office expanded to meet new and heavy demands, which reached their peak in 1972, when 7,800 staff were employed.

The second main theme of the HMSO story is how the Department has fostered new technology, particularly in the last twenty years or so, taking full advantage of the development of the computer not only to enhance management capability but to improve its printing Presses and the distribution of the nearly 50,000 titles which are held in its Publications Centre. Innovative developments in electronic printing and publishing are imminent.

The third strand has been the gradual evolution of a more dynamic business style in response to both external and internal pressures, notably the new-found freedom of customers to buy elsewhere and the move to an arms-length relationship with them. The resulting pressures, coupled with more concentration on mainstream activities, have led to a gradual reduction in the size of the Office to 3,400 or so. But far from demoralizing staff, the businesslike way in which this major rationalization was accomplished has led to a better organized and more confident organization which stands ready to meet whatever further challenges may emerge.

Mr Barty-King has done well to distil the main essence of how Her Majesty's Stationery Office has developed over these last 200 years. I am proud that it falls to me as the Controller and Chief Executive of the day to pay tribute to the considerable achievements of the Department over the years and to the continuing excellence of the staff which has made those achievements possible.

WILLIAM SHARP
Controller and Chief Executive
January 1986

# PART I

## 1786 — 1900

### Why His Majesty's Stationery Office
### needed to improve His Majesty's stationery

Brooks's, June 26th 1830

So poor Prinney is really dead – on a Saturday too, as was foretold.
. . . I have just met our great Privy Councillors coming from the
Palace – Warrender and Bob Adair included. I learnt from the
former that the only observation he heard from the Sovereign
[William IV] was upon his going to write his name on parchment,
when he said – 'You have damned bad pens here'.

THOMAS CREEVEY
*MP for Thetford, to his step-daughter Elizabeth Ord concerning the
swearing in of the new Privy Council on the death of King George IV
and the succession of his brother.*

### Why the Stationery Office
### message of economy found willing ears

I object to having tons of papers which are never opened sent to my
lodgings. I have been out of town for a few weeks, and on my
return, instead of being able to go to the Derby I had to wade
through a mass of Parliamentary papers. I put away 1 lb and threw
away about 2 cwt. I could not sell the residue; I could not exchange
them for books, for that would be selling them; I could not burn
them, for that would be voted a nuisance. Why should these tons of
paper be thrust on unwilling members?

MR V. SCULLY
*MP for Cork County, in Commons debate on Civil Service Estimates,
1 June 1865.*

# CHAPTER 1

# An agency
# which customers repaid

## 1786 – 1823

*Mr Mayor points the way*

Britain in the 1780s, perhaps like Britain in the 1980s, was undergoing major changes in its industries and no less in its institutions and social structure. The struggle was neither short nor easy. Parliament had resisted passing legislation to free the Government of 18th-century Britain from the dead hand of privilege for six years. Amateur, aristocratic administrators, who owed their appointments to court influence and kept them by royal favour, knew that none would dare question the tradition by which they exploited their 'patents' to bring the greatest private gain. Their confidence was justified however only so long as events outside the palaces in which they wasted so much of their time did not put the King in need of very much more money than Parliament was prepared to vote him.

Suppression of the revolt by the colonists of British North America and preservation of the First British Empire were the top priorities for George III and justification for the continuation of his 12 years of personal rule. But the money was running out. Concede the American colonists their independence, the Whig opposition urged Lord North, and end the war you cannot afford. The first phase of the war against the colonists had ended with surrender at Saratoga in October 1777, and now the French were coming to the aid of the 'Americans' for what they hoped would be the kill. In his last appearance in the House, the dying Lord Chatham asked for one last effort or 'let us fall like men'. So be it, said the Whigs, but if Britain is to continue the war, let

3

alone win it, then the money to do so must be found by economies spread over the whole spectrum of public administration, and particularly in the unproductive Royal Household. In 1779 associations were formed demanding economy, and petitions poured into Westminster.

Edmund Burke, the 'Irish adventurer' with the brilliant oratorical skill, the Whig MP for traditionally Tory Bristol, rose from the Opposition benches on 11 February 1780 to seek leave to bring in a Bill 'for the better regulation of his Majesty's civil establishments and of certain public offices; for the limitation of pensions [sinecure appointments] and the suppression of sundry useless, expensive and inconvenient places [for MPs]; and for applying the moneys saved thereby to the public services'. He was reflecting the mood of the nation at large but his private Bill was savaged in committee.

At the end of 1781 news reached England of General Washington's victory at Yorktown, but Lord North insisted on continuing the war. He was forced to resign however on losing a vote of confidence on 19 March 1782, and was succeeded by the Marquess of Rockingham who formed a Whig Coalition ministry which included Edmund Burke as Paymaster. The terms on which the Whig leader agreed to form a Government were peace abroad and economy in all public offices at home.

At Rockingham's request Burke re-introduced, this time as a Government Bill, his Plan for Economic Reform which aimed to abolish some 40 places of profit under the Crown filled by MPs, and reduce too the Government's patronage of sinecures. The Bill just had time to get on to the statute book before (on 1 July 1782) Rockingham died of influenza, only three months after taking office. Burke was excluded from the ministry which Lord Shelburne formed on 11 July to take the place of Rockingham's; but as Paymaster once again in the ministry which the Duke of Portland formed on 24 February 1783 after Shelburne's resignation, he was responsible for a second piece of legislation:

*An Act for establishing certain Regulations in the*
*Receipt of His Majesty's Exchequer*

Whereas it appears, from the Reports made by the Commissioners appointed to examine, take, and state the Publick Accounts of the

Kingdom, that in the Receipt of His Majesty's Exchequer there are several useless, expensive and unnecessary Offices; and that the Emoluments arising from other of the Offices in the said Receipt of Exchequer are become excessive; and that the Mode of paying the Officers by Allowances, Fees and Gratuities is inconvenient both to the Publick and to Individuals: for Remedy whereof, be it enacted . . . That the several Offices of the Two Chamberlains, the Tally Cutter and of the Usher of the Exchequer, shall, from and after the Death, Surrender, Forfeiture or Removal of the present Possessors of such Offices respectively . . . be abolished.

The office of Usher of the Exchequer was held by Horace Walpole, youngest son of Sir Robert Walpole who was Britain's first 'Prime Minister' and had retired in 1742 as the Earl of Orford. Author, prodigious letter-writer and Member of Parliament through the influence of his father, Horace Walpole had obtained sinecure offices worth £5,000 a year. Incapable and unwilling to carry out the duties of patent-holder as Usher of the Exchequer, he farmed them out to deputies whom he paid generously. They included having to shut the gate of the Exchequer office each evening and the furnishing of:

paper, pens, ink, wax, sand, tape, penknives, scissors, parchment, and a great variety of other articles, to the Exchequer, Treasury, and their offices, and to pay the bills of the workmen and tradesmen who serve those offices.

The sand was for sprinkling on paper to dry wet ink. He would also have furnished the sand box to be found on every desk to contain it. The pens would have been swan or goose quills imported from Russia or Germany. 'Dutching' quills needed considerable skill and was probably part of the patentee's service. This meant clarifying and hardening them by removing the tough outer skin on the barrel of the feather so as to leave the transparent surface, and pulling out the pith by plunging it into heated sand and drawing it across a knife. For further sharpening the writer used the 'penknife' which Walpole also supplied. The tape was for binding up bundles of papers. For some reason it was dyed a delicate shade of pink, but became known as red tape. When he went to pay the attorneys Dodson and Fogg, the 'rascally pettifogging robbers' who had landed him in the Fleet

Prison, Mr Pickwick saw Fogg pull a bundle of papers from his
pocket and walk to the window:

> 'There's no occasion for Mr Pickwick to move, Mr Perker', said Fogg,
> untying the red tape which encircled the little bundle, and smiling again
> more sweetly than before. 'Mr Pickwick is pretty well acquainted with
> these proceedings '
> *The Pickwick Papers* by Charles Dickens

The protracted procedures of lawyers and Government officials
came to be symbolized by the red tape which held the
voluminous paperwork together, and according to *Brewer's
Dictionary of Phrase and Fable* Charles Dickens was responsible
for introducing the term in this sense. When, during the Great
War of 1914–18, they had difficulty in obtaining the obligatory
pink dye the tape was white, except in the Royal Courts of
Justice.

Horace Walpole was at pains to justify the profit he made out
of his monopoly:

> Many of the articles specified are stated in a very ancient table of rates in
> the Exchequer (I think of the time of Edward the Third, so that my office
> is, if a grievance, no very novel one); and, on those, large profits are
> allowed to the Usher, whence my profit arises, and whence, if it is largely
> augmented of late years, a candid examiner will observe that that increase
> proceeds from the prodigious additional consumption of paper, pens,
> ink, wax, which the excessive increase of business at the Treasury must
> occasion; and therefore, should a much less quantity of those implements
> be employed, my profits would decrease in proportion. When, therefore,
> I am charged as receiver of 4,200 $\ell$ a year, it should be remembered that
> though I was so in the year 1780 (though I shall show that even that is an
> arbitrary statement not calculated on any medium), yet I cannot equitably
> be reckoned communibus annis to receive so large a sum. I have shown
> that 1,800 $\ell$ a year was the medium on twelve years, and those not of my
> last receipts.
>
> *Memoir relative to his Income* by Horace Walpole

The Duke of Portland, the new First Lord of the Treasury and
head of the Government, set about enacting the provisions of
Burke's Receipt of the Exchequer Act without delay; and on 25
July 1783 instructed John Mayor of the Treasury to find out all he
could about one aspect of it, 'an intended reform of the

stationary'.* Mayor considered that the first piece of information he needed was what public offices had been paying patentees for their paper and pens, and to this end he obtained the permission of the Treasury to ask each of them to send him their stationery bills for the year 1782. When he got them he had a clerk copy them all into a ledger.

On 13 December he was told by the Duke of Portland to wait on Lord John Cavendish to take final instructions on whether he was to proceed with his plan of reform from Christmas onwards. He was given an appointment for 19 December, but two days previously the Portland ministry fell and the meeting never took place.

So, to put the new administration formed by Lord Chatham's son William Pitt the Younger in the picture regarding his plan, on 30 December 1783 he wrote a memorandum to the Lords Commissioners of the Treasury from 3 Suffolk Street summarizing what he had done so far and seeking authority to take the further action which would set the plan in motion. The Duke of Portland and their Lordships, he said, had approved his plan for reform and wished him to put it into operation. He reckoned that a 'Nett Saving will be made of more than £30,000 per annum'. Sir William Chambers of the Office of Works, asked whether conveniences could be found in the New Buildings at Somerset House for the proposed operation, had reported that they were all appropriated. Chambers had looked at both the Salt Office and the Lottery Office but neither of them was worth repairing.

Mayor recommended their Lordships to rent a place for not more than £200 a year until a fit place could be found in Somerset House. Many of the contracts which public offices had with patent holders, he said, were on the point of expiring, so if there was to be a change in the system after Christmas they wanted to know about it.

On a separate sheet he set out a list of the offices whose

---

* The word was spelt this way in all official documents for some years. Some goods were bought from an itinerant vendor who continually moved from one village to another; others were from a retailer in a permanent shop which was static or stationary, and such items, particularly books, newspapers and writing materials, acquired the name 'stationary' or (later) 'stationery' goods.

agreements with their stationers were determinable at certain periods. He had one success to report however:

> Mr Walpole the Patentee, to serve the Treasury and Exchequer, has consented to give up his Patent for such a compensation as the Lords of the Treasury should think reasonable, by the means of which (allowing a handsome compensation) a saving will be made of more than the expense calculated for the reform of the whole.

That, said John Mayor, was the situation to date. Could he have their instructions as to what to do next?

On the second sheet of his memorandum to their Lordships he set out his proposals:

> The Plan to reform the abuses found to subsist by extravagant charges of stationary is to Establish an Office under the management of a Comptroller from which every Office and Person entitled to be supplied with stationary is to be served.

He estimated the Office's annual expense would be:

> Comptroller for himself 5 p$^r$cent upon the Nett savings made by the Office, but not to exceed one thousand pounds (or settled at a thousand as shall be best approved) and fifteen hundred pounds for the following Assistants or Persons necessary to be employed therein:
> Deputy or Chief Clerk     Six Porters
> Four Clerks               Two Carmen
> Three Journeymen          Keeping 3 horses including Farrier
> Incidental expences including necessary woman, coals, candles, stationary, etc.

When a whole year went by without hearing from their Lordships, John Mayor wrote another memorandum on 20 December 1784, this time from Dean Street in Soho, to Sir George Rose, Clerk of the Parliaments. Having done everything in his power towards preparing for carrying into execution the plans which he had had the honour of recommending to the Lords of the Treasury for reforming the abuses in the Stationary, he begged:

> that you will make known to their Lordships my request that I may have any appointment to controul the same, without which I am not properly authorised to obtain from the public offices such information as will enable me to provide for serving them, and that their Lordships will also

> give me such orders to provide a place for the business, till one should be
> ready in the new buildings at Somerset House, and for Stocking the same
> as shall seem meet and proper to their Lordships.

What had caused the delay? The 24-year-old Prime Minister
had more urgent matters on his mind, not least of which was
surviving the constant defeats he suffered in the House of
Commons (where he was the only Cabinet Minister) from the
Opposition of Charles James Fox, ten years his senior and
Britain's first 'Foreign Secretary'. But winning the general
election of March 1784 with a large majority gave Pitt new
confidence, and within a year he was anxious to emulate Edmund
Burke's crusading zeal to reform the public service by appointing
commissioners to examine abuses in a further list of offices. In
Shelburne's ministry, after all, he had been Chancellor of the
Exchequer 'at two and twenty – it is some glory!' as Horace
Walpole had remarked.

The extravagant charges being made for stationery were among
the abuses which Pitt sought to remove. The fact that a plan
already existed to effect that aspect of reform, and was in the
course of being implemented, apparently got lost in the broad
sweep of the youthful new broom. That no one at the Exchequer
Office had seen fit to bring to the attention of the First Lord of the
Treasury John Mayor's memorandum of 30 December 1783,
with the appended 'Plan' which the Duke of Portland, a previous
First Lord, had so heartily approved, may be surprising, but can
alone account for Pitt's Commission on Fees having stationery on
their agenda. Their first report, dated 11 April 1786, stated that
the expense of stationery appeared to them excessive 'which we
attribute to the circumstances of that article being supplied by
patent'. This was a state of affairs which led them to wonder
'whether a more eligible plan might not be adopted for furnishing
Offices with the necessary article'. But by then events had
overtaken them.

By the end of July 1785 the Lords of the Treasury, after seven
months deliberation, had decided to give John Mayor's Plan a
try. In a letter of 5 August 1785 the Treasury directed Sir
William Chambers of the Office of Works to prepare an estimate
for the fitting up of a 'Stationary Office' on the east side of New

Palace Yard. On submission it was accepted, and a woman called Ann Grey (or Guy) was hired as Housekeeper at £60 a year from 10 October 1785 'for herself and to keep a Maid'. Though occupied from this date, the premises were not formally leased by the Crown till 1792. Ann was in the building alone with her domestic for six months, though doubtless there was eventually much toing and froing of workmen bringing in office furniture, laying carpets and hanging lamps, to say nothing of loading up the floor with stocks of stationery. It was not till 5 April 1786, however, a week *before* the publication of Pitt's Commissioners' Report, that John Mayor was at last given the 'controul' he asked for by being appointed not Comptroller (as designated in his Plan) but 'Superintendant' of a new Department within the Treasury called His Majesty's Stationery Office.

## Mr Pitt takes action

The establishment of the Stationery Office provided for a Comptroller (of Accounts) but the post was not filled. It was second in the line of command to the Superintendent and carried an annual salary of £200 compared with John Mayor's £600. In fact his deputy and principal assistant was a Chief Clerk, Joseph Weston, who also got £200 a year. His staff varied from the list he gave in his Plan but not to any great extent. He had two Principal Warehousemen, four Clerks, three Parchment Cutters (at a guinea a week), two Porters and a Watchman, besides the Housekeeper who had taken up her duties six months before. Their total salaries and wages amounted to just over £2,000 a year.

Although the establishment dated from the beginning of the financial year 1786, William Pitt as First Lord of the Treasury did not have an opportunity to set the wheels turning until 15 August 1787, when he chaired a meeting at Treasury Chambers with Sir John Aubrey and a Mr Eliot. The Treasury minute of this meeting put the record straight:

> The Article of Stationary being an object of considerable Expenditure in the several public offices, My Lords have had under their attentive

consideration an Arrangement for supplying the same in the most economical and convenient Manner to such of the said offices or to the Departments thereof as are now served under Patents or Contractors for Terms of Years; and are of Opinion that it will be expedient to adopt the following Establishment and Regulations for the present, a proper Warehouse, Office and other conveniences having been already provided for the purpose under their Lordships' directions.

The establishment was as stated, and at the end of the list the minute added 'As the Business increases My Lords will consider of the Propriety of allowing more Journeymen and Porters'. Readiness to adapt to changing circumstances was the order of the day from the very first, and flexibility, the ability to move with the times, became the permanent guideline throughout the years ahead.

In setting up a centralized service to effect economy and convenience, the Government's main concern was to make it as prompt as the one which customers received from the patentees, if not more so, and one which gave them the items they required of high but not over-costly quality in a way that did not compete unfairly (because subsidized) with commercial suppliers (manufacturers and wholesalers). With the removal of the profiteering patentee who bought cheaply and sold at outrageously high prices in the safety of his monopoly, they did not want to be seen to be substituting any other form of middleman. So their first regulation was:

> that every article to be bought of the Maker when that can be done, and at the usual Credit given to Wholesale Stationers. Each Article is to be charged at Prime Cost; no arbitrary Price to be permitted. The several offices to pay the Amount of six months Expenditure in advance, which it may reasonably be supposed will enable a sufficient provision for each.

Thus the Office was acting as the agent of those Government offices whose arrangements with patentees Mayor was able to terminate or had expired, and who paid for the items out of their own Vote at cost, plus a percentage of the value of the stationery ordered to cover the salaries and running expenses at New Palace Yard. To enable him to purchase the initial stock before the money started coming in, Mayor had to provide sureties under Treasury orders for £6,500. The annual value of the stationery to be supplied was put at £17,000, and the 'levy' on this paid by customers was reckoned to be 37 per cent in 1789, though by 1797 it had come down to 15 per cent. Mayor listed 60 articles including quill pens and sand boxes.

The Stationery Office was not ready to offer a service to its first customers until the autumn of 1787, or perhaps even December. Some were supplied wholly, others only partially. A note in the minute of 15 August 1787 reads:

> Acquaint Mr Stephens, for information of the Lords of the Admiralty, that a proper supply of Stationary will be ready to be delivered at Christmas next at the office in New Palace Yard appointed for the purpose of supplying all the public offices . . . The officers of the Admiralty, Treasurer of the Navy, Navy Office, Victualling Office, the Sick and Wounded Seaman's Office to provide themselves with required articles from this office; also the Lord Chamberlain, Lord Steward [both members of the Royal Household], the Paymaster General, Comptroller of Army Accounts, Commissioners of Taxes, Commissioners of Salt, of Hackney Coaches, of Hawkers and Pedlars, of Stamps.

At that date there were 11 offices on the books of the Stationery Office, for the supply of which imprests (advances of money) were ordered to be issued by the Treasury. But it also supplied stationery to both the House of Lords and the House of Commons. By 1797 when Horace Walpole, then the Earl of Orford, died, and the patent of Usher of the Exchequer expired with him, John Mayor was partially supplying the Treasury and Exchequer; the Secretaries of State for the Home Office, the Foreign Office, Aliens, War and Colonies; the Post Office, Customs and Excise Office, Ordnance and the Chelsea Hospital. The growth of business was determined by the expiry dates of the patents. Though freed from the tyranny of the patentee, a public office was not compelled to buy all or part of its stationery requirements from New Palace Yard, but could negotiate with suppliers of its own choosing and purchase from them directly. But in their second report of 1788, the Commissioners on Fees forecast a reduction of 40 per cent in the stationery bills of those who ordered through the Stationery Office, so the incentive to buy from John Mayor was considerable. Economies were estimated at £50,000 a year.

Although in 1786 the post of 'Comptroller of Accounts' under the Superintendent was left vacant, it was later filled by Lewis Wolfe who in 1798 took over control of the whole operation from John Mayor with the title 'Comptroller' instead of 'Superintendant', which with that of 'Comptroller of Accounts' was never revived.

With the expiry of the last of the patents in 1800, new regulations were issued instituting an improved method of keeping the accounts and directing that all stationery requirements should be procured from the manufacturers at wholesale prices. In 1806 the Treasury ordered that the buying by the Stationery Office of paper, parchment, pens and sealing wax should be by public and open competition, and that the lowest tender should be accepted in every case – a rule extended to *all* forms of stationery in 1812. The Comptroller had to advertise for sealed tenders to be submitted on days named in the advertisement for articles of precise quality and specification. Samples of what was required were open to public inspection.

The Comptroller's control over his staff was tightened when in 1807 the Treasury authorized him to report 'any case of Disobedience or Neglect which may occur; and even to suspend from their functions, and Mulct [deprive of] their Pay, such Persons as shall wilfully disobey or carelessly neglect to execute the Orders duly given to him'. The business was increasing and the number of staff with it. The establishment of 1807 was a Comptroller and three Clerks, a Cashier and two Clerks, a Storekeeper and four Clerks, a Receiving Clerk, Parchment Clerk, five Warehousemen, three Assistant Warehousemen, three Order Clerks, Parchment Sorter, three Parchment Squarers, two Paper Cutters, two Carters, six Porters, a Messenger, Watchman and Housekeeper. Each member of the staff had a personal copy of the new regulations of 1807, on the front page of which was printed:

> Mr . . . . . . . .
> I hereby strictly enjoin you to attend carefully to your Duty as directed by the Rules contained in the following Regulations, so far as you may be concerned.
>
> . . . . . . . . Comptroller

In an age when bribery and corruption were commonplace, it was necessary to have a rule which laid down that:

> No Persons employed in the Stationery Office shall in any manner be interested in the manufacture or purchase of stores, nor shall receive any Fee or Gratuity more than his Salary on Pain of Dismission from his Office.

And no 'Coals, Candles, Oil, Turnery Wares or other Articles' were to be issued except for use in the office or a warehouse. There were rules for the Comptroller, too, who was enjoined to:

> investigate carefully the Prices paid for the several Purchases in order to ascertain whether they are as low as Articles of the like Nature and Quality are bought at from the manufacturers by wholesale Stationers.

Since 1802 the Comptroller had been George Dickins, later to be questioned by investigators whose rigorous examination as to his honesty gave him a fit of apoplexy, and his behaviour may already have warned his masters at the Treasury of the need for more precise regulations of the kind they introduced in 1807, the year in which the Stationery Office's service to its customers was enlarged to include the ordering of printing, which extended the area of potential temptation.

These customers did not include the Houses of Parliament. The supply of paper for, and the printing of, what were known as 'Parliamentary Papers' continued to be handled by the Speaker of the House of Commons who contracted the work out to commercial 'Parliamentary Printers' who had the monopoly. With the advent of Irish MPs to Westminster on the union of the Irish and British Parliaments in 1801, the volume of Parliamentary Papers greatly increased and the printing of them became a regular rule. They were only for the eyes of Members, however, not the general public, and distribution was according to the list recommended by the Committee for Promulgation of the Statutes which reported in 1801.

With the creation of a Stationery Office, Speakers began to look to it for advice on how to have printing done more cheaply, and from March 1810 sent their bills to New Palace Yard for examination. In 1810 a scale of prices for Parliamentary printing was fixed by the London Master Printers. It covered only the routine papers needed for the daily working of the Commons such as its Journal, Votes and Bills. No official report was made of what was said in the debates, which Members regarded as strictly privileged and for their ears only. In 1738 both Houses had denounced the newspapers for daring to print what they claimed to be reports of debates. It was a bold step therefore for William Cobbett to start writing, as he did in 1802, summaries of debates in both Houses as a supplement to his *Political Register*, available to anyone prepared to buy a copy. He gave even greater offence with his purported verbatim accounts of speeches in the Lower House, under the title *Parliamentary Debates*, the first volume of which came out in 1804. From 1807 Cobbett entrusted the printing of these to Luke Hansard's* son Thomas Curson Hansard who, in 1812, took over the whole operation.

In this year George Dickins and his staff, now grown to 44, moved from New Palace Yard to New Scotland Yard. The Comptroller's control over his staff became lax, and Dickins himself soon succumbed to tempting offers which became more rewarding with every new responsibility. When the allegations being made that stationery supplied by his office was being sold to private individuals became too strong and too frequent to ignore, the Government had to act, and in 1822 appointed a Select Committee to investigate them.

Henry Jennings, who in 1820 had petitioned Parliament demanding that one office only should undertake *all* Government printing and save £50,000 a year, told the Committee sarcastically he well knew· that 'the Stationery Office people, and the public and Government printers, would be able to satisfy the Committee through the medium of falsehoods and official terms as to their innocence, purity, merit and utility; and it is most easy for them to do so from the very nature of the business of both stationery and printing'.

---

* By a happy coincidence the present headquarters building of HMSO in Norwich is adjacent to St Mary's Church where a plaque records:
  Luke Hansard 1752–1828.
  Baptized in this church, served an apprenticeship in Norwich as a printer, went to London in 1774 and began printing the journals of the House of Commons.

In the course of enquiries other abuses came to light. A Mr Ready, the Keeper of the Treasury Board Room, for instance, had been selling Stationery Office paper to his tailor to pay for his suits; Sir Matthew Bloxham, the Storekeeper at New Scotland Yard, had been discounting bills for Stationery Office contractors; Dickins himself was found to have borrowed money from contractors in return for who knows what favour. Unsuccessful wholesale stationers and printers told the Committee of their great dissatisfaction with the way contracts were arranged. Evidence was given too of alleged misappropriation of official paper by printers for their private work.

The Select Committee on Printing and Stationery of 1822 recommended a Treasury review of the Stationery Office establishment and this was conducted by Alexander Young Spearman. The Committee felt the principle of a centralized purchase and supply organization was the right one, and were opposed to any reversion to the old system of Departments buying their own stationery. Indeed it expressed its disapproval of those public offices which still insisted on doing this.

When the Stationery Office had recently disputed the quality of paper supplied, arbitrators had settled the matter; and in his report Spearman recommended that the system should be applied to similar disputes about *all* stationery supplies. He also suggested detailed changes in contract arrangements for parchment, paper, printing, binding and small stores. But his main recommendation was that instead of collecting payments from each Department, which had become too cumbersome, the Stationery Office should have its own annual Vote of money from Parliament, from which all the stationery and printing it supplied should be paid. The probable expense of providing stationery, printing and binding for certain public Departments for the year 1824–25, when the new system was to start, was put at £59,760, of which £5,068 was for salaries. Spearman thought the staff should be reduced from 40 to 32, and the Office divided into two branches, the Comptroller's for purchase and the Storekeeper's for receipt and issue.

In the minute attached to Spearman's report, dated 21 March 1823, the Treasury condemned the irregularities revealed by the

Select Committee, accepted Spearman's ideas for reform and directed that *all* Departments should henceforth obtain stationery, printing and binding from the Stationery Office. It quoted the passage in the Select Committee's report in which they stated:

> that it appears that some public offices still continue to procure Articles of Stationery from Private Tradesmen and *strongly recommend that the whole supply of Stationery for the public service should be made in one and the same manner* under whatever arrangement it may be thought fit to adopt.

The Lords of the Treasury agreed. They considered it fitting that the stationery used in public Departments should be all of one pattern and to that end there should be only one source of supply. So they instructed the Comptroller to:

> Write to the several Public Departments to communicate to them the desire of My Lords that in future all supplies of Stationery, Printing and Binding may be procured from the Stationery Office only, and that no private Tradesmen whatever may be employed for any article which can be procured through that Department.
>
> Transmit to them at the same time a List of Articles which will in future be supplied by the Stationery Office, and acquaint them that My Lords will forward to them patterns or descriptions of those articles, it being their Lordships desire that the patterns and qualities of the articles should be the same for all Departments and that no article should be supplied of a different pattern or quality except upon a requisition from the Head of the Department requiring it . . .

The 38 years in which customers paid for the stationery and printing of their own choice had come to an end, though the use of the word 'still' in the report of the Commons Committee would seem to indicate that by 1823 those who elected to buy other than from the Stationery Office were in a minority. The 1824 Vote was to supply 33 Departments. Their printing requirements were to be put up for three-year contracts to firms who had been master printers for at least a year. The lowest tender was to be accepted, and the work done on the cheapest possible quality of paper. The 'list of the articles to be supplied in future by the Stationery Office' was as follows:

| | |
|---|---|
| Paper | Binding, Ruling, etc |
| Parchment and Vellums | Almanacks |
| Printing | Court Calendars |

Court Guides  
Directories  
Messenger Bags  
Cards  
Erasers  
Hones  
Ferrett [a stout cotton or silk tape]  
Laces  
Black Ink  
Red Ink  
Ink stands   – Glass  
   do         – Pewter  
   do         – Lead  
   do         – Ebony  
India Rubber  
Ivory Folders  
Lead pressers  
Pasteboards  
Pounce* and Boxes  
Card Boards  
Pencils  
Pens and Quills  
Cord  
Rulers  
Wax  
Wafers  
Strops  

Scissors  
Wafer Boxes   – Tin  
   do         – Paper  
Wafer Seals  
Despatch Boxes  
Bramah's Pens and Holders  
Tape  
Memorandum Books  
Seal Engraving  
Copper Plate Printing  
Portfolios or Blotting Books  
Packing Cases  
Ink Casks  
Leather Bags  
Army and Navy Lists  
Statutes  
Files   – Pasteboard  
   do   – Wire  
Silk Cord  
Needles  
Pins  
Marking Ink  
Japan Ink  
Leather Straps  
Sand  
Sand Boxes  

It was the first major revision of the arrangements introduced by John Mayor in 1786; and financing by Vote without repayment stood the test of time, and of social, economic and political change, for the next 156 years – a continuity which every year gave its service increased authority.

* Pounce was a fine powder such as pulverized sandarac used to prevent ink from spreading in writing over an erasure or on unsized paper, and also to prepare the surface of parchment to receive writing.

1. Horwood's Map of Whitehall of 1792 (above) includes the sites of the Stationery Office's locations at New Palace Yard, New Scotland Yard, and Princes Street.

To the Right Honorable the Lords Commissioners
of His Majesty's Treasury

My Lords

In consequence of an intended Reform in the
Stationary I received his Grace the Duke of Portlands
Orders on the 25th of July last to get such information as I
thought necessary thereto. I found that an Official letter from
the Treasury to the Public Offices was necessary to obtain Copies
of their Stationers bills for the Year 1782. These accounts were
sent to me as they came in, which I have thoroughly inspected
and one of the Clerks that I intended employing in the Office
is now Copying them into a Ledger (some of them being but lately
sent me) and from them I am able to report to your Lordships
that should the Plan which the Duke of Portland approved
(a Copy of which I transmit herewith) meet with your Lordships
approbation and I have the honor of being continued in the
execution of it a Nett saving will be made of more than £30,000
Pr Annum. Sir Wm Chambers was desired to report if Conveniencies
could be found in the New Buildings at Somerset House suitable
for such an Office as I thought necessary for the purpose. He
returned an Answer that the Buildings there were all appro-
55                                                priated

2. John Mayor had been instructed to produce a plan for reforming the supply of
Government stationery following the Receipt of the Exchequer Act. Two days before he was
due to meet Lord John Cavendish to agree the implementation of the plan, the Government
fell. A fortnight later he wrote (above and overleaf) to the new Lords of the Treasury in an
effort to get his scheme off the ground.

To the Right Honorable the Lords Commissioners
of His Majesty's Treasury


My Lords

In consequence of an intended reform in the
Stationary, I received his Grace the Duke of Portland's
Orders on the 25th of July last to get such information as I
thought necessary thereto. I found that an Official letter from
the Treasury to the Public Offices was necessary to obtain Copies
of their Stationers bills for the Year 1782. These accompts were
sent to me as they came in, which I have thoroughly inspected
and one of the Clerks that I intended employing in the Office
is now Copying them into a Ledger (some of them being but lately
sent me) and from them I am able to report to your Lordships
that should the Plan which the Duke of Portland approved
(a copy of which I transmit herewith) meet with your Lordship's
approbation and I have the honor of being continued in the
execution of it a Nett saving will be made of more than £30,000
per Annum. Sir Wm. Chambers was desired to report if conveniencies
could be found in the New Buildings at Somerset House suitable
for such an Office as I thought necessary for the purpose. He
returned an answer that the Buildings there were all appropriated

to particular Offices. After which he was desired to view with me the Salt Office and Lottery Office neither of which were found worth repairing. I had therefore recommended to rent a place which was not to exceed £200 a year till some fit place should be found either in the New Buildings or some one of the Offices vacated to go there. Saturday the 13th Instant I received the Duke of Portlands orders to wait on Lord John Cavendish to take His final instructions to proceed on the Reform from Christmas. I was to have been with Him on the 15th. It now rests with your Lordships, and therefore I thought it my duty to take as early an opportunity as I could to acquaint your Lordships with the exact situation of the business for there are so many of the Public Offices whose agreements with their Stationers (at certain prices) continue only till a year or Six Months notice is given to dissolve them. Mr. Walpole the Patentee to serve the Treasury and Exchequer has consented to give up his Patent for such a Compensation as the Lords of the Treasury should think reasonable by the means of which (allowing a handsome Compensation) a saving will be made of more than the expence Calculated for the Reform of the whole. I hope to receive your Lordships instructions how I am to proceed. I am my Lords

Your Lordships most Obedient
Humble Servant
John Mayo

Suffolk Street (No 3)
Decr. 30th. 1783.

to particular Offices. After which he was desired to view with me the Salt Office and Lottery Office neither of which were found worth repairing. I had therefore recommended to rent a place which was not to exceed £200 a year till some fit place should be found either in the New Buildings or some one of the Offices vacated to go there. Saturday the 13th instant I reced the Duke of Portland's orders to wait on Lord John Cavendish to take His final instructions to proceed on the reform from Christmas. I was to have been with Him on the 19th. It now rests with your Lordships, and therefore I thought it my duty to take as early opportunity as I could to acquaint your Lordships with the exact situation of the business as there are so many of the Public Offices whose agreements with their Stationers (at certain prices) continue only till a year or six months notice is given to dissolve them. Mr. Walpole the Patentee to serve the Treasury and Exchequer has consented to give up his Patent for such a Compensation as the Lords of the Treasury should think reasonable, by the means of which (allowing a handsome Compensation) a saving will be made of more than the expence Calculated for the reform of the whole. I hope to receive your Lordships instructions how I am to proceed. I am my Lords

Your Lordships most Obedient

& Humble Servant

John Mayor.

Suffolk Street (No. 3)

Dec: 30th, 1783.

Whitehall Treasury Chambers 15th August 1787.

Present

Mr Pitt
Mr Eliot
Sr John Aubrey

Read and approved the Minutes of the last Board.

The Article of Stationary being an object of considerable Expenditure in the several public offices, My Lords have had under their attentive Consideration an arrangement for supplying the same in the most aconomical & convenient Manner to such of the said offices or to the Departments thereof, as are not now served under Patents or Contracts for Terms of years; and are of Opinion that it will be expedient to adopt the following Establishment & Regulations for the present, a proper Warehouse, Office & other Conveniences having been already provided for the Purpose under their Lordships Directions.

## Establishment — The Salaries to be paid clear of all Deductions whatever.

Mr John McMayor Superintendant .................................... P Annum — £600 ... from 5 April 1786.

Comptroller ................................................ do — £200 from

Joseph Weston _ Chief Clerk ............................ do — £200 from 5th april 1786.

Thos Hitchcock from 5 April 1786 & Pierce Temple from 10 Octobr 1786 } Two principal Warehousemen, one in the Paper & one in the Parchment Branch at £150 P Ann: each ............ } £300 —

John Tull from 5 July 1786 } Two Clerks at £100 P annum each ............ £200 ...

Willm McKraith } One do — at £70 P Ann: from 5 April 1786 & An Order Clerk at £100 P ann } £170 —

Three Parchment Cutters at one Guinea a Week each to be appointed by the Superintendant } £163.16 —

John Francis from 5 April 1786 } Two Porters at £40 P Annum each ............ £80 ...

John Whitehead from 10 June 1786 } One Watchman _ at £40 P Ann: from 5 July 1786 _ Housekeeper Ann Guy for herself & to be paid £60 P ann: from 10 last 1785 } £400 ...

As the Business increases, My Lords will consider of the Propriety of allowing more Journeymen & Porters.

A Cart & two Horses for conveying the Stationary to the Public offices; to be charged at the Expence which shall be actually incurred for the same.

3. Although the Office was set up from the beginning of the 1786–87 financial year, the Prime Minister, William Pitt, as First Lord of the Treasury did not have the opportunity formally to approve the new Department until 15 August 1787. The official Treasury minute is reproduced above.

PRESENT  Mr. Pitt
Mr. Eliot
Sir John Aubrey
READ and approved the Minutes of the last Board

THE ARTICLE OF STATIONARY being an object of considerable
Expenditure in the several public offices, My Lords have had under their
attentive Consideration an Arrangement for supplying the same in the
most aconomical & convenient Manner to such of the said offices or to
the Departments thereof, as are not now served under Patents or Contracts
for Terms of years; and are of Opinion that it will be expedient to adopt
the following Establishment & Regulations for the present, a proper
Warehouse, office & other Conveniencies having been already provided for the
Purpose under their Lordships Directions.

ESTABLISHMENT – The Salaries to be paid clear of all
Deductions whatever

| | | | |
|---|---|---|---|
| Mr. John Mayor | Superintendant ...................................................... per Annum | | £600 .. from 5th April 1786 |
| | Comptroller ........................................................... | Do. | £200 .. from |
| Joseph Weston | Chief Clerk............................................................ | Do. | £200 .. from 5th April 1786 |
| Thos. Hitchcock from 5 April 1786 – & Pierce Tempest from 10th October 1786 | Two principal Warehousemen, one in the Paper and one in the Parchment Branch at £150 per Ann: each ................ | | £300 ....... |
| John Tull – from 5th July 1786 | Two Clerks at £100 per Ann: each .......................... | | £200 ....... |
| Willm. McKraith | One Do. at £70 per Ann: from 5th April 1786 & An Order Clerk at £100 per Ann from | | 170 ....... |
| | Three Parchment Cutters at one Guinea a Week each to be Appointed by the Superintendant | | £163... 16.... |
| John Francis from 5th April 1786 – & John Whitehead from 10th June 1786 | Two Porters at £40 per Annum each ...................... One Watchman – at £40 per Ann: from 5 July 1786, Housekeeper Ann Grey for herself & to keep a Maid £60 per Ann: from 10 Octr. 1785 | | £80 ....... £100 ....... |

As the Business increases, My Lords will consider of the Propriety
of allowing more Journeymen & Porters.

A Cart & two Horses for conveying the Stationary to the Public offices;
to be charged at the Expence which shall be actually incurred for the
same.

4. The location of the Stationery Office in New Palace Yard, Westminster, between 1785 (when it was first occupied) and 1812, was on the east side, which included the Waterfront Buildings shown in this 1808 drawing.

5. In 1812 the Stationery Office moved from its first home in New Palace Yard to New Scotland Yard, seen here in a print of 1766.

6. The Stationery Office was divided by Alexander Spearman's reform plan of 1824 into two sections, one at James Street, the other at Whitehall Place. It was reunited under one roof in 1856 at Storey's Gate.

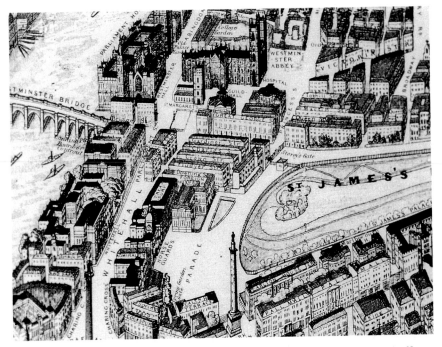

7. The location of Storey's Gate is shown in this 1851 illustration. The actual offices were next to the Westminster Hospital in the wrongly spelt Princess (Princes) Street.

8. Parliament had traditionally regarded their debates as privileged and for their ears only. It was a bold step therefore for William Cobbett, pictured above, to start publishing texts of speeches in his *Parliamentary Debates*.

9. Luke Hansard of Norwich, from a portrait hanging today in the Office of the Editor of *Hansard* in the Palace of Westminster. His son Thomas took over Cobbett's *Parliamentary Debates* in 1812.

10. Messengers of the Vote Office, who each morning delivered Parliamentary Papers to the houses of MPs living near the Palace of Westminster, posing for a photograph in 1885.

11. Controller William Greg personally tried the new 'Type-Writer' in 1876. He was not impressed. Machines such as this Sholes and Glidden typewriter, made by E. Remington and Sons in 1875, were not easy to handle.

12. By the time this drawing was made in 1887, the Treasury had accepted typewriters as useful pieces of office equipment. At first they typed only capital letters. In 1900 there were two machines in the Stationery Office.

# FIRST REPORT

OF

# THE CONTROLLER

OF

# HER MAJESTY'S STATIONERY OFFICE.

Presented to both Houses of Parliament by Command of Her Majesty.

LONDON:

PRINTED BY GEORGE E. EYRE AND WILLIAM SPOTTISWOODE,
PRINTERS TO THE QUEEN'S MOST EXCELLENT MAJESTY.
FOR HER MAJESTY'S STATIONERY OFFICE.

1881.

[C.–2782.]   *Price* 2½*d.*

13. In 1881 the Treasury asked Sir Thomas Digby Pigott to submit a report on the establishment, duties, expenditure and receipts of the Stationery Office.

CHAPTER 2

# Financed by Parliamentary Vote without repayment

## 1824 – 1855

*Divided but expanding*

The division into two branches, for purchase and for receipt and issue, was not only operational but physical. When the new arrangement started in April 1824 the Comptroller and his staff were in James Street off Petty France overlooking St James's Park (now Buckingham Gate) and the Storekeeper was at 5 Whitehall Place. Total staff numbered 44, not the suggested 32.

When George Dickins died of the apoplexy which seized him after his gruelling time at the hands of the Select Committee, the Treasury appointed the 29-year-old Alexander Spearman, the author of the new plan, as Comptroller in his place, though only for a year. The future baronet was transferred to Treasury duties before the move from Scotland Yard, and the post given to John Church.

There is no record of the action taken by John Church when he heard of the condition of a vital piece of His Majesty's stationery at a critical moment on the first day of William IV's reign, but doubtless it was traditionally prompt. 'So poor Prinney is really dead – on a Saturday too, as was foretold', wrote Thomas Creevey to his step-daughter Elizabeth Ord on 26 June 1830 from Brooks's, about what happened at the swearing in of the new Privy Council:

> I have just met our great Privy Councillors coming from the Palace – Warrender and Bob Adair included. I learnt from the former that the only observation he heard from the Sovereign was upon his going to write his name on parchment, when he said – 'You have damned bad pens here'.

19

Within six years Church was seeking to expand his empire in the direction of Parliamentary printing. Luke Graves Hansard had come under attack from a Select Committee in 1828 over paper supply; and Joseph Hume had attacked the whole concept of a single King's printer. In 1831 Church wrote to Hansard, the Commons printer, telling him that he had been ordered to report on his paper and on his accounts. He also wrote to Spottiswoode, the Lords printer. He thought the Stationery Office could supply paper to the Parliamentary printers of both Houses at a lower prime cost. He was ordering paper on a large scale, and this called for open competition. Some 30 per cent of the current cost could be saved. And 25 per cent could be saved by adopting a fixed price scale for all Parliamentary printing, as for Departmental printing.

Church's prying certainly frightened Hansard. Lobbying John Rickman, Assistant Clerk of the House of Commons, for support in February 1831, he pointed out 'the danger that might befall us if the Stationery Office were to act under any order of the Treasury and procure a stock of paper, and then pounce on us with an imperative order to use it'. When, at Church's request, Hansard met the Stationery Office Comptroller, he described him in his journal as 'a wily man, in which quality I do not attempt to cope with him. I keep a straightforward course, I hope Providence will help me'.

The spirit of Edmund Burke was abroad once more. The Reform Bill was passed in 1832; and the 'ruthless and inquisitive' Reformed Parliament, as Hansard called it, was out for retrenchment at any cost. But, the printer told yet another committee, 'Mr Church may give what opinions he pleases, but I assure you that we will not print at his prices'. In his journal for 18 June 1832 he wrote: 'Church made a furious attack on me and the manner of arranging House of Commons printing. It is plainly his endeavour to work up some plan for getting the whole control of the business into his hands.' It was in fact that the London printers Nichols should print the Votes for both Houses, and Spottiswoode the Bills and Journals, both under Stationery Office supervision. Hansard refused to justify to the Comptroller his charges for nightwork, Sunday work and corrections. When he heard that a Select Committee had approved Church's plan for 'compressed' printing, he declared 'the effects will be to us most terrible'. The proposed new format and type would make Hansard's equipment obsolete 'at a stroke'. His firm would be deprived of its safe monopoly and become one of several printers whom the Stationery Office might think proper to employ. He did not lack supporters however. 'Mr Church may have some very sharp people to look after among his contractors for cheap stationery,' said one of them, 'and he may have imbibed the opinion that tradesmen are rogues, and will cheat if they can; but it is very unfair for any person to insinuate so foul a charge against such respectable persons as Messrs Hansard without having some grounds for the insinuation.'

The fight over the supply of paper was even more bitter. It raged briefly round the notorious Sir John Key, MP for the City of London, who was concerned with several contracts for supplying paper to the Stationery Office up to 1832, and his son Jonathan, who in 1833 contracted for paper worth £50,000. John Church had appointed the latter his Storekeeper at £400 a year without knowing he was Sir John's son. A newspaper called *The Age* made allegations of the 'corrupt system of management' at the Stationery Office which a Select Committee however refuted. On 16 August 1833 the Committee declared the evidence 'had left a favourable impression upon their minds with respect to the general good management of the Department and of its utility to the public'.

Both the printing and paper supply issues had reached deadlock when in 1834 fire destroyed the Palace of Westminster in the worst conflagration London had seen since 1666. The inevitable surrender (under the inevitable protest) of the printers and paper contractors to the will of the Treasury and its agent His Majesty's Stationery Office was only delayed, not halted; and the controversy switched to the equally thorny matter of who was to be allowed to *read* Parliamentary Papers. Up to 1836 they were not available to the public, being the private property of the printers who had the monopoly for producing them. Even Jeremy Bentham could only obtain a copy of a Bill or an issue of a House of Commons Journal through a friendly MP. But the

conclusions of the three reports on Parliamentary Papers written
by the radical, ex-India nabob Joseph Hume were formulated in
16 resolutions, which the House of Commons passed on 13
August 1835 – in spite of the Government's attempt to postpone
them. The most important was that Parliamentary Papers should
be made accessible to the public by purchase at the lowest price –
that is, the cost of running off additional copies, not of
typesetting. In 1836 the 'Sale Office' of the House of Commons
was established and Messrs Hansard, as printers to the House,
were put in charge of it, taking any profit in abatement of their
printing bills.

This was a major change of attitude, and that it was long
overdue was recognized by the Select Committee on Printed
Papers who admitted:

> Your Committee consider it difficult to estimate the extent of the injury
> either to the Government or to the community at large by the limited
> circulation of the Acts of the Legislature which, in consequence of the
> existing monopoly, are placed in the hands of comparatively few persons,
> and thus imperfectly made known to the bulk of the people.

At the same time a minor change took place with the Vote for
Parliamentary Printing being united with that for General
Stationery and Printing. The total amount for that first year 1835
was £195,856. The combined operation had increased because
of changes in servicing other parts of the United Kingdom. In
1830 the office of King's Stationer in Ireland had been abolished;
the following year supplies for Irish Departments had been added
to the Stationery Office Vote; and in 1832 a branch of the
Stationery Office had been opened in Dublin. In 1833 came the
surrender of the office of King's Printer and Stationer for
Scotland.

In his 12 years of control, John Church had brought lasting
changes to His Majesty's Stationery Office. One of his final tasks
was to ensure that on the death of King William IV on 20 June
1837 none of the many hundreds of pieces of print for which he
was responsible slipped by with a 'His' instead (for the first time
in the history of the office) of a 'Her', in the designation of the
young Queen Victoria.

### *For* Her *Majesty's Government*

John Church may have seemed wily to Luke Graves Hansard, but his cunning, it seems, did not extend itself to persuading the Treasury to augment his salary of £600. His frequent applications for a rise were always refused. But his successor of 1838, John Ramsay McCulloch, according to his friend Thomas Murray, employed greater tact. 'He memorialized the Treasury for an increase to the salaries of his inferiors but preferred no petition to his own income.' The Treasury acceded to his request and the beneficiaries thanked their master for his action by presenting him with two elegant, silver claret decanters. But the real prize was the increase to his own salary which followed.

John McCulloch was a convivial Scot 'with a sort of boyish gaiety of spirit', a literary man who was briefly editor of *The Scotsman* newspaper and an academic who in 1828 had become Professor of Political Economy at University College, London. The author of works such as *Principles of Political Economy*, *A Treatise on Taxation* and a *Commercial Dictionary*, he had been given a literary pension by Sir Robert Peel of £200 a year.

Such a man could be expected to take the duties of Comptroller of the Queen's Stationery Office in his stride – and with relish. His salary, as Thomas Murray explained, was 'exclusive of an official residence, coal and candle', and an allowance for attendance. 'The situation of the house (overlooking St James's Park) is as good as any in London.' House and office were all one. More than three-quarters of the large amount of space was taken up by the latter. The residential quarters comprised a drawing room and study on the middle floor; his 'business room' as Comptroller on the floor above, which the family used as a dining room on the 'great occasions' when they entertained formally; and on the top floor the kitchen – which made it a long run downstairs for servants answering the front door bell. It was 'a berth which lasts *ad vitam aut culpam* without regard to change of Ministers'.

But he was only 49 – born in the year of the French Revolution – and though Thomas Murray got the impression that the labour was light ('not perhaps averaging an hour, or at most two hours a

day, often not five minutes'), he took the job with due seriousness
and applied his fertile mind to ways of solving the various
problems he had inherited from John Church with attack and
imagination.

Getting the Treasury to review the salaries of his 'superior,
well-educated' staff involved a recommendation that they should
be divided into four pay-scales ranging from £90 a year to £350 a
year, with the exception of Mr Rapley, Examiner of Printers'
Accounts, who he thought was worth £375. The reclassification
plan, which had been submitted after the staff had presented the
new Comptroller with a claim for higher wages, was accepted.
With the Office now serving 166 Departments, the increases had
come none too soon. In the knowledge of the loyalty of a
professional staff whose expert advice he would have to rely on
for most of the questions referred to him by the Treasury, he was
able to turn to a matter more in his field as a man of letters – libel.

With Parliamentary Papers being sold to the public –
'published', that is, in the technical sense of the word – their
contents were no longer 'privileged' as far as libel was concerned
(as statements inside the Chamber were). The year before
McCulloch became Comptroller a man called Stockdale had sued
Hansard in the Queen's Bench for a statement in a Government
publication which he claimed libelled him, and won. In ruling
that Parliament was just as answerable to the law of libel as any
private individual, the courts were setting a precedent. In 1840
the House of Commons vindicated itself by passing the Parliamentary Papers Act to give summary protection to anyone
employed in their publication.

Of even more interest to McCulloch was the matter of the
distribution of the nearly 200-year-old *London Gazette*. As
Comptroller of Her Majesty's Stationery Office he had no juris-
diction over this, but did supervise the accounts for printing and
publishing the *Dublin Gazette* which was produced under patent.
When the patent for the *Edinburgh Gazette*, which had been
launched in 1793, expired in 1847, the accounts of that publication came under his notice also. In June 1848 he was asked
by Charles Trevelyan, an Assistant Secretary at the Treasury,
to investigate the organization behind the *London Gazette*.

Arrangements had been made by the Government for printing and publishing an official gazette with a summary of home and foreign intelligence before 1665, the year in which the first single-sheet issue with no title was produced when the court happened to be in Oxford to escape the Plague. There was no statutory authority for its production, but it had a monopoly of all official news for 33 years – until 1698, when it remained a convenient vehicle for many kinds of public information. The editor or 'gazetteer' was appointed by the Home Office and Foreign Office in turn.

In 1848 the Treasury directed that the accounts of the *London Gazette*, which had a large revenue from advertisements, should be seen by the Stationery Office, and that at the end of that year its profits should be paid to the Exchequer. The Treasury agreed to McCulloch's suggestion that its printing should be put out to tender; and the contract was won by Harrison & Sons who had been its printers from 1756 to 1790. When he advised, as an economist, against reducing its selling price he was overruled. The lower price failed to attract more readers and the circulation remained around 400.

But if the print run of the *London Gazette* was static, that of the 600 or so other Parliamentary Papers published every year had reached ungovernable proportions. Any MP or peer could get almost anything printed merely for the asking. Eccentrics with views on topics of little interest to anyone other than themselves could have them aired at the public expense in the form of wordy petitions. Some 15,258 Parliamentary Papers on every conceivable subject were issued between 1801 and 1834. Enough were always printed of each paper for every MP and peer, every public office and the whole list of subscribers – whether they wanted them or not. Readership for the 1,331-page return giving the names of school teachers will have been limited but it was given the full print run, and cost £4,016. The same applied to the 938-page volume costing £1,591 giving the names and characters of West Indian slaves.

John McCulloch's evidence to the Select Committee on Miscellaneous Estimates, of which the most expensive portion was the £121,000 for printing these Papers, was drawn to the attention of another committee which in 1850 was the latest to investigate the mounting cost of what was printed 'by Order of the House' under the wing of the Speaker. It was largely due, they found, to the 'very great alterations which have taken place in the last Twenty Years in almost all Laws relating to property, to persons and the institutions of the country'. But many Papers were of ephemeral interest only, such as the one relating to the State of Religious Disputes in Madeira. They recommended reducing the print run of each Paper to 1,000 of which 938 went to the Vote Office, leaving only 62 for sale and store.

There could be no such easy way of reducing the cost of the Stationery Office's service, the demand for which flatteringly rose. Between 1839 and 1856 the number of customer Departments increased from 169 to 269, and the value of stationery supplied from £260,000 to £500,000. The Treasury cannot but have been pleased at this demonstration of its offspring's popularity but, as ever, made sure that the rate of expansion was kept as low as possible.

One way was for the Stationery Office to make money as well as to spend it. Up to 1841 waste paper was the 'perk' of office keepers and messengers who disposed of it for what they could get. But on several of them being caught in the act, the Civil Service had no alternative but to be seen to condemn 'systematic misappropriation of public property' as 'objectionable and illicit'. The culprits were brought before the magistrates and sentenced. There was too the security angle; and a Treasury minute of 1852 pointed out that the practice seriously compromised the safety of public records. In future 'waste paper and old articles of stationery of every kind must be collected and delivered to the Comptroller of the Stationery Office at the end of each half year, to be sold by him on behalf of the public'. Ten years later the income from the sale of waste paper paid for the combined salaries of the Comptroller and the clerical and professional staffs of the Stationery Office in England and Ireland – £13,400.

The buying of the material so much of which became 'waste' needed more expertise than the purchase of the ordinary stationery items which the Stationery Office supplied. In 1841 an Examiner of Paper, with the ability to apply scientific tests to it, was appointed and in his first year is reported to have saved £10,000. This was the fore-runner of the HMSO Laboratory which in the 1980s tested a vast range of supplies, prepared specifications and advised on supply items of every kind except machinery.

## *McCulloch's undivided authority*

Sir Alexander Spearman's idea of giving the Stationery Office two heads, a Comptroller and a Storekeeper, and two branches, had never worked, and in 1856 the separate office of the latter was abolished, and another Clerk First Class appointed to perform newly specified store-keeping duties. The Comptroller was re-invested, after 33 years, with 'undivided authority and responsibility of the whole office'. The total establishment was reduced from 69 to 55, but the cost to the Treasury of the salaries and wages of the smaller staff was higher – £12,748 instead of £9,764. They received pay rises every year instead of every five years. But they had to work for their extra remuneration. Revised rules introduced in 1856 stated there would be no extra payment for extra hours of attendance. Clerks and Examiners must report *before* ten in the morning so that every branch could start work at that hour. But, with half an hour for lunch between one and half past, they went home at 4.30. To the 1807 rule against employees having an interest in a stationery manufacturer was added:

> It is indecorous and inexpedient that the Examiners of Papers, Printing and Binding and Small Stores . . . should be intimately connected with contractors or tradesmen employed by the Stationery Office . . . It would be liable to misconstruction and suspicion.

A Binding Branch (vellum and leather) had been established in 1847, and a binding expert became part of the Stationery Office's staff from 1849 and within a year reduced binding expenses by £18,000. Small Stores were paper and parchment, pins and sealing wax. They continued to be bought under yearly contracts after 1856, but, to ensure proper quality, the purchase of pens and knives from that date had to be put out to tender from an 'office list' of respectable tradesmen after enquiries had been made regarding their substantial character.

The practice of giving regular contracts to one printer for the wide variety of forms required by Government Departments was also discontinued in 1856 when the current contract expired. In its place John McCulloch introduced a new form of agreement with several 'respectable' printers in London by which each was bound to produce for stated prices whatever he was asked for. Another office list of 'Job-Work' printers was kept of those 'willing to tender for, and who are believed to be equal to, the Government work'.

No one was more conscious of the need to move with the times than John McCulloch. He objected to employing any printer for a fixed term, because, he said, no one could foretell how things would stand after five or seven years. New printing inventions might be introduced in that time. He should be able to give any printer six months' notice. Respectable printers should not be deterred from entering into such an agreement. If they behaved honestly and did the work properly, they would not be capriciously interfered with:

> The work is executed at the lowest rates by willing parties who know that the moment they attempt to make an overcharge, or otherwise misconduct themselves, or execute their work in a slovenly manner, or take to do it more time than is required, they may expect to receive six months' notice, or less.

The Comptroller had never had power to interfere capriciously or otherwise with the printing of what since 1811 had been called *Hansards Parliamentary Debates*, still unofficial and unrecognized. But in June 1855 he was directed by the Treasury to subscribe for a hundred copies to distribute to public Departments and to post to India and the colonies. Up to then there had been irregular subscriptions from certain offices amounting to 35 copies only, but the introduction of Her Majesty's Stationery Office as distributor gave the publication official status of a kind hitherto denied it.

John McCulloch's views on the amount of talking done in Parliament are not on record, but he joined his predecessors (and successors) in being appalled by the amount of Government printing, and added his voice to the clamour for its curtailment. He suggested that any Member who wanted a manuscript to be printed should have to obtain the approval of a small committee of MPs and the Librarian of the House. He also advocated confining to the narrowest limits 'the practice of what is called *Confidential* printing' – charged at the higher rates. Latterly it had been carried much too far, 'many papers being treated as confidential that might without inconvenience of any kind be stuck up at Charing Cross'.

It was one of the last McCullochisms to be delivered from those comfortable offices in James Street off Petty France, which then overlooked St James's Park. Whitehall Place and James Street were abandoned, and John McCulloch moved as supremo into the offices which had been made for him and his staff of 55 out of Queen Anne's Royal Stables at Storey's Gate, Princes Street.

# CHAPTER 3

# At Storey's Gate

## 1856 – 1900

McCulloch, whose salary range was raised from £800–1,000 to £1,000–1,200, had William Ginger, Chief Clerk, as his second-in-command, a team of Clerks of first, second, third and fourth class, two Examiners of Printers' Accounts, a Receiver of Printed Forms, an Examiner of Binding, an Examiner of Paper, warehousemen, messengers and porters. On the establishment was a Clerk First Class in charge of stationery in Dublin, where there was also a statute Warehouse-Keeper. David McCulloch (the Comptroller's son?) was Storekeeper of Educational Works in Dublin.

The offices at Storey's Gate served the Stationery Office for nearly a century. In all that time they cannot have changed to any great extent, and probably the description of them in 1900 written by Arthur Hammond, who joined the Stationery Office as a 20-year-old junior clerk in that year, would have been recognizable to one of John McCulloch's young men in 1856:

> The most impressive parts were the two entrances with their somewhat imposing stone staircases between a tall archway with massive iron gates leading to a large cobbled courtyard with a round granite water trough for the royal horses to quench their thirst. Most of the stabling doorways were closed in and the interior accommodation adapted for office and warehouse areas. What was it all like? Pretty awful – antique, even the office furniture was old-fashioned and grubby. I happened at one time to work in a room in a passage with well-worn wooden flooring (no covering of any sort) with the notches sticking out! . . . Lavatories were old-fashioned and smelly – altogether a dirty place, the scent of which pervaded our room. There was no washing accommodation. Shelves were taken out of cupboards in rooms, a wash basin let in and a pail

underneath and a can of water. Often office floors were flooded from basin overflows. No one seemed to care, I suppose because nothing much could be done except complete evacuation which occurred a long time after. One room at least had been in occupation by Old Scotland Yard pending the opening of the New Scotland Yard on the Embankment. It housed all the lethal weapons used by murderers and the like. At one time I occupied that room with others. No ghosts however!

What kind of office accommodation John McCulloch had at Storey's Gate is not clear – nor whether part of it served as his residence. From 1877 the Controller received an allowance of £300 'in lieu of a residence'; but E.H. Chapman, who became a clerk there in 1899, tells of Mr Wilson the Office-Keeper serving not only the office 'but also the domestic requirements of the Controller who had a suite of residential rooms as well as his private office in a locked enclave in the centre of the first floor'.

The level of luxury, or otherwise, behind those sealed doors has never been revealed, but if it even approximated the 'Articles Required for the New Room, Mr Cuthbertson (HMSO)' of which an undated, handwritten copy has survived, he must have been very comfortable. Mr Cuthbertson was obviously anticipating a range of activities of a surprisingly catholic nature with a distinctly musical bias. At the head of the list was:

> 1 Piano (Broadwood's preferred)
> 1 Trombone

and further down:

> 1 copy Hallelujah Chorus
> 1 tuning fork
> 1 quire Music Paper.

For his sustenance he ordered:

> 1 Liqueur Stand        1 Saucepan (for Beans)
> 1 Claret Jug           1 Potato Steamer
> 1 Grog Kettle          1 Copy Beeton's Cookery Book;

for his health:

> 1 Asthma Kettle;

for his toilet:

> 1 Dressing Case Fitted
> 1 Tooth Brush (secondhand, if new are not allowed).

Or is the document a joke, the satirical invention of a Victorian hoaxer with a down on the Civil Service in general and the Stationery Office in particular? Probably. It could have been written by one of the office clerks whose free issue extended no further than pens, pencils and erasers which, if John McCulloch had had his way in 1861, would have been commuted to an allowance to save the Treasury £7,000 a year. But, perhaps because it would have proved more generous to clerks' pockets than the public purse, the Treasury had still not taken up the idea when three years later John McCulloch died.

*Greg's ordinary instrumentality*

His successor in 1864 was another literary man, William Greg, who was equally concerned for the well-being of his staff. When two years later he found that porters frequently died without leaving enough money either to maintain their families or pay for their own funeral, he had sixpence a week deducted from their 27s a week wages and invested in a trust for their dependants' benefit. Greg did not anticipate objection to so moderate a payment 'which is designed simply to promote their welfare and respectability'.

He was also shocked to find the prevalence at Storey's Gate of 'the pernicious practice of borrowing money', often at exorbitant rates of interest, from professional money-lenders. It had landed more than one person in serious pecuniary embarrassment approaching insolvency. He issued a grave warning in 1866 that such circumstances made it impossible to be an efficient or trustworthy public servant. He would recommend the Treasury to suspend or dismiss any delinquent who accepted accommodation bills or gave promissory notes.

Trustworthiness and reliability had to be the keynotes of a service with which customers would only be satisfied so long as they could take its smooth running for granted, and not be made aware of it by continual hitches. The justification for not allowing public offices to make their own purchases directly was still the saving of taxpayers' money. But in doing that, it was still essential that the existence of a Government central purchasing office should not be seen to be 'unfair' to the trade.

William Greg made priority of assuring the Treasury in 1872 that in buying paper, the Stationery Office's chief article, he called for tenders from a large number of 'qualified and reliable tradesmen, thus ensuring the full benefit of competition, and then accepting the lowest tender'. He bought quills, ink and stands in the same way; but steel pens and pencils directly from the makers at large discounts. For printing and binding 'we feel the market, and test the lowness of our prices by inviting competition afresh from time to time'.

Open competition by advertisement had been abolished in 1860 when the Treasury sanctioned competition by invitation. In this way only the 'qualified and reliable' whose firms were known to be able to meet the requirements of the Stationery Office were invited. Compulsory acceptance of the lowest tender remained for some time but it too was eventually abolished to enable the Stationery Office to make a best buy to achieve an optimum saving – the arrangement which has persisted to the 1980s.

Greg was well aware that, to succeed, a Comptroller had to master the art of keeping staff, customers and the trade happy – and the Treasury at bay. The yardstick was the number of new customers who applied for the service each year. In 1861 the Stationery Office had taken over the printing of Admiralty Charts from the Hydrographic Department. Some who had used the service had been abolished, such as the Lottery Office (1810), the Registry of Slaves (1820), the Marshal of the Marshalsea Prison (1841), the Commission for French Claims (1845); but ten had become customers in 1867, including the British Museum, seven in 1872 and 12 in 1873, including the Railway Commission, Greenwich Naval College and *Ross's Parliamentary Record*. (In 1866 the Government had given a Mr Ross a grant of £400 a year to supply 200 copies of the weekly *Ross's Parliamentary Record*, which in 1868 was reduced to £200 for 100 copies.)

The build-up of faith in the Stationery Office's ability to deliver the goods was certainly gratifying. But the Comptroller would have been even more gratified if more of them had a Clerk of Stationery 'competent and well-paid' who was able to check his Department's stationery demands *before* submitting them to Storey's Gate. Every day Greg's Chief Clerk queried the quantity or quality of five or six requisitions, and insisted on changes which kept their effectiveness but halved their cost. There was no incentive for customers to keep their requirements cheap, and the Stationery Office was in no position to give them an account of what their demands had cost at the end of the year, because no record was kept of Departmental expenditure, only total Stationery Office expenditure.

For all Greg's success in satisfying staff, customers and trade, he found himself in mounting disagreement with the politicians. He considered it would be most injurious to the public interest to impose fines and penalties on defaulting contractors, as a Select Committee suggested in 1874. 'At present' he told them 'we never have a dispute, scarcely even a difference of opinion that cannot be settled in five minutes conversation.' Contractors obtained 'strict justice' and made their offers in the knowledge that there would be no arbitration and no appeals. He only imposed fines for late delivery (to enforce punctuality); never for defective or inferior quality, which he merely rejected and left the contractor to re-offer at a lower price.

Greg told them some saving might come from taking away distribution of Parliamentary Papers and Government publications from the printers and giving it to the Stationery Office who would run a central depot for the purpose, but the division of responsibility would bring constant 'irregularities' and wrangling over whose fault it was when something went wrong:

> The Committee had in their minds some vague idea, not thoroughly worked out, that generally all Government and Parliamentary work should be done by, and not merely through the Stationery Office . . . [who] should actually sell them over the counter, not merely arrange for their publication and sale through publishers and booksellers.

He saw the process ending with the setting up of 'one vast printing establishment for Government purposes':

> I need not point out that this would be a movement in an entirely opposite direction to that hitherto pursued and generally urged with much zeal by

reforming Members of Parliament, namely that Government should do nothing itself that it can safely and well get done for it by the ordinary instrumentality.

### Electric pen or typewriter?

The Comptroller was obviously taking the side of the trade, as all his predecessors had done, and this spurred his interrogators to heckle him with even greater ferocity – and the suspicion lingered that his championing their case was not entirely altruistic. Greg was not driven to apoplexy by the Select Committee on Public Departments (Purchases, etc) of 1874, as George Dickins had been by an earlier ordeal, though his calm was severely shaken by them. He had recovered it however when two years later he was called upon to judge how seriously to take the potential of an American invention for mechanized writing.

Christopher Latham Sholes produced the first successful typewriter in 1873. Was it the most important development since printing, or a contraption with as little a future as the steam motor car or the semaphore telegraph? Unwilling to be seen to be backing a loser, Greg was at first sceptical of the piece of ironmongery which printed letters by type worked by a piano movement being made by Remingtons in the USA. After receiving several requisitions for one of the machines, he told the Treasury in March 1876 that he had endeavoured to form a judgement of the probable utility of them by personal inspection and enquiry, and had obtained the views of official gentlemen who had tried them in actual operation. He had to confess he was not inclined to estimate highly their practical value.

After spending nine months thinking it over, the Treasury agreed that typewriters should not be placed on the Stationery Office's 'list of approved articles', but sanctioned the purchase of two machines for a trial at Inland Revenue. Then in 1877 their Lordships took the matter out of Greg's hands by appointing a Committee of Enquiry into the usefulness of several recently developed contrivances, including Zuccato's Patent Papyrograph and the Edison Electric Pen, which were both basically copying machines.

The reaction of the Civil Service to the invention of the typewriter was in line with that of business and commerce in Britain. It was seen primarily as a quicker method of making readable copies of a hand-written document. Only a very few offices of any kind had typewriters before the 1880s. By 1886 the Treasury had accepted them as essential pieces of office equipment, mainly (as ever) on the grounds of their saving labour and so money – a skilful female machinist could produce 45 words a minute, doing the work of two copyists and saving two-thirds of the wages. The Treasury ruled that requisition of machines by public offices should be through the Stationery Office, which was instructed to consult their Lordships however about each application. Though seen as a long-term money-saver, at twenty guineas each machine was expensive – at a time when a Writing Assistant who copied documents accurately, quickly and legibly could be had for a pound a week. The cautious approach to full use of the machine throughout the public service was understandable. It only typed in capital letters, the line of writing could not be seen by the operator, and any errors had to be removed by scraping with a sharp knife and the correction inserted either by hand or by re-positioning the paper on the machine. It was only when the so-called 'visible' machines appeared, where the line of writing could be seen, and the shift mechanism was introduced, that typewriters really came into their own. By 1889 the Stationery Office was being allowed to supply typewriters without reference to the Treasury.

It was a period of innovation too in the 400-year-old processes of letterpress printing. *The Times* was trying a new method of typesetting; another printer was doing it by electricity; a Dr Mackie had patented yet another system. Would the Government's use of any of these inventions save taxpayers' money? Had the time come, perhaps, to do away with the separate departmental Presses at the Admiralty, War Office, and the Science and Art Department where procedures and disciplines varied, and establish a Central Printing Press near the public offices, under the supervision of the Comptroller of Her Majesty's Stationery Office, to which they would all have direct access for confidential and urgent work? Those who reported to the Treasury in July

1877 thought it had, but few agreed with them. They did not believe that the Government should be their own printers and wanted the work still to be done under contract by the trade.

No one was more aware of the need to leave technical work to technicians than William Greg – indeed he made a virtue of being 'non-technical'. In a Comptroller of the Stationery Office he contended it was an asset. When the 1874 Committee had recommended uniting control of the Stationery Office and the management of the *London Gazette* (and other *Gazettes*) 'under one officer, possessing the requisite technical knowledge of stationery and printing', Greg agreed it would put the Comptroller less in the hands of his Examiners. But, he said, these men were expected to do their duty with integrity and practical skill. A 'professional' Comptroller was unlikely to get the business done either more cheaply or better. A Comptroller's job included scrutinizing official demands, cutting them down where excessive, inducing the officers of various Departments to forego them if unnecessary and insisting on them being executed in a more economical form, and the judging of cases when urgency warranted ordinary rules being set aside:

> It is not very easy to believe that a Practical Printer could exercise the same influence and possess the same firmness in carrying out his purpose as a gentleman more socially and intellectually the equal of those with whom he has to argue and whom he may have to withstand – it is not easy to convey the desired meaning without phrases of a kind that may be thought unseemly.

Greg need have had no complex about his lack of technical training. Even the technical men were known to get it wrong. In 1879 R.S. Culley, Engineer-in-Chief of the Post Office, declined the offer of Colonel Reynolds, Alexander Graham Bell's representative in London, to demonstrate the Canadian's 'telephone', for in his view the possible use of the invention was 'very limited'.

### Non-technical Digby Pigott

When Greg died in 1877 there was surprise in some circles that the Government did not follow the resolution of the Commons

Committee of 1874 that, when the position of Comptroller next fell vacant, it should be filled by a person with the requisite knowledge of printing and stationery. For they decided to offer the post to a Treasury clerk named Thomas Digby Pigott who was Parliamentary Secretary to Lord Northbrook. Moreover he owed his selection, it was hinted, to the friendship of his father, the vicar of Hughenden, with the Prime Minister, Benjamin Disraeli, now Lord Beaconsfield, whose Buckinghamshire parish that was. The appointment had the bad smell of patronage about it. The Commons reacted by passing a resolution calling for the resignation of Digby Pigott, who was known outside his Civil Service duties as an authority on bird life and was later to find a luminous owl. Disraeli disclaimed any knowledge of the man or that he had been helped by him in his electioneering campaign. He did not even know Digby Pigott by sight and believed he had voted against him in the last general election.

In a long and witty speech to the House of Lords in July 1877, Disraeli not only justified the appointment of Digby Pigott but the non-appointment of the type of man favoured by the Committee of 1874, whose resolution seemed to him far from practicable. He could not undertake the responsibility of appointing someone who had retired from business and from whom business had retired. The salary offered would not attract a man at the top of a commercial printing house. The job required considerable administrative ability, official experience and a capacity for labour. He could not ask a decayed printer or stationer, a retired or unfortunate tradesman, to fill a post of this character. He had not advertised the vacancy in the newspapers or proclaimed it at Charing Cross, but 'let it be known'. Six names had been placed before him and he had chosen Digby Pigott's. He did not feel himself justified in accepting the resignation of the man chosen in the way he had described – and the Treasury clerk's appointment was confirmed.

Tom Digby Pigott's capacity for labour proved phenomenal – and for enlisting the help of those who were authorities in their own spheres. Within two years he had reorganized the Stationery Office on the lines recommended for the Civil Service as a whole by the Playfair Commission in 1874. He made the old establishment, except Staff Officers, redundant, with a view to replacement by Lower Division Clerks, and the creation of a Higher or Directing Branch. He appointed an Assistant Controller (the title began to be spelt thus from this time), and divided the non-professional staff into three branches under an Accountant, Registrar and Demand Clerk, and Storekeeper. The professional staff consisted of a Superintendent of Printing, an Examiner of Paper and an Examiner of Binding, each with a team of technical subordinates. The reorganization of 1879 represented a saving of £4,000 a year in salaries. The annual cost of the old establishment was £14,515; that of the new £10,327.

Digby Pigott called for a review of the existing policy of placing the publication of official books 'either in a single hand or selecting a publisher for separate groups of works'. It appeared very doubtful to him whether the present system did not minimize the inducement of publishers to push Government (non-Parliamentary) publications. The 50 distributors were agents only, and they had no catalogue of Stationery Office books, only a series of lists. He called the Treasury's attention to the high prices paid for House of Commons printing, which in 1880 resulted in the awarding of new contracts to Hansards for Commons Papers and Journals, and to Eyre & Spottiswoode for those of the Lords, which showed considerable savings.

Any economies Digby Pigott could effect now made more impression on the nation's overall expenditure if only because of the greatly increased Stationery Office Vote. That first sum of £60,000 had grown to £460,000 in 1880. *All* business connected with printing, binding, publication or the supply of stationery for the public service was transacted at Storey's Gate. And it was not just business generated by Vote customers; considerable work for instance was being done for the India Office on repayment terms. Gross expenditure in 1879–80 was £568,377.

Perhaps because of the circumstances surrounding his appointment, the Treasury asked Digby Pigott to write them a report on establishment, duties, expenditure and receipts – which they had never asked from any of his predecessors – with the promise that a Committee of both Houses would examine him on it. This first report was a wide-ranging document of 17 printed pages dated

January 1881, to which he attached an appendix on the Office's origin and growth, written by H.G. Reid, Assistant Controller, and a list of customers from 1787 to 1880, indicating the year in which they first took the service. They came to well over 300.

He was not asked for views, only for facts. He gave the former, when asked, to the Sherbrooke Committee of both Houses. In the light of their recommendations in 1882 the Commons had all Parliamentary printing laid open to contract except the *Votes and Proceedings*. Hansards and Eyre & Spottiswoode, the Commons and Lords printers respectively, became agents of the Stationery Office instead of Parliament. All Parliamentary Papers from then on were kept in a single store controlled by the Stationery Office, whose agents sold all of them. Proceeds went to the Exchequer.

Thus in 1882 Her Majesty's Stationery Office could be said to have become (in a very restricted sense) a 'publisher'. By the end of the decade it had become responsible for the conduct of the *London Gazette*, and 'printer to Her Majesty of all Acts of Parliament, and holder of royal copyrights'.

More and more books were published at the public expense which would never have been issued as private speculations – books such as the encyclopedic report of the voyage of HMS *Challenger* on ocean life, which cost £53,500. The Stationery Office would lose if any private person could reprint such a book for his own profit without breaching copyright. An enterprising printer in Ashton-under-Lyne, for instance, had brought out *Regulations for Musketry Instruction*, which was a blatant imitation of the official War Office booklet. As Digby Pigott told the Treasury, the circulation of this unofficial and possibly incorrect manual might lead to results more serious than the loss of public money. 'A mistake in a book of Bugle Calls or Signals – to take an instance happily unlikely but not impossible – might involve disasters on the field.'

### *Printer to Her Majesty*

When the Treasury saw that in the ten years 1873–83 the Stationery Office's expenditure had increased by 27 per cent –

from £432,500 to £549,100 – they wanted to know why, and asked Henry Fowler MP to find out. In his report of 1884 he said the reason was an increase in Stationery Office *business* of 60 per cent. This was largely attributable to the increased business in public Departments, and had it not been for 'proportionate economies' would have been much larger.

Digby Pigott came out well from the Fowler Committee hearing and emphasized the fact in the second report he wrote for the Treasury in 1887. As their Lordships would see, the Stationery Office had not attempted to make any innovation except on principles which had received clear Parliamentary sanction:

> Recommendations of Committees, however wise and strongly urged, are of little use, more especially when clashing with vested interests, unless some Department or individual is responsible for carrying them into effect.

The Stationery Office had had no direct responsibility for the printing and sale of Parliamentary Papers, and the result had been 'a wholesale waste of public money'. But when the Stationery Office was given that responsibility by the Treasury and Parliament in 1882, 'the recommendations of Committees, the wisdom or necessity of which had never been questioned but which had remained dead letters for years, have without any friction or difficulty been carried into effect'.

The year after the Fowler Report (1885) the Office of Works transferred the sale of Ordnance Survey Maps to the Stationery Office, though the Director-General of the Survey continued to do the surveys and the maps.

It was not only Government Departments but the House of Commons who were making more work for the Stationery Office. Sessions had grown lengthier, and there were more debates in Committee. Reports of debates had grown from 4,400 pages for the year 1877 to 8,500 pages for 1881. When Hansards asked for a proportionate increase in their subsidy Digby Pigott took the opportunity of exposing what he considered their extravagant charges. In 1878 they had proposed producing fuller *Parliamentary Debates* for £20,540, but Digby Pigott's experts had told him that 'at any reasonable estimate' the Government could do the work itself for half the amount. 'The comparison is interesting as another illustration of the profits which Government monopolists have felt justified in claiming and have commonly claimed successfully.'

With a Lords Committee in 1888 declaring the system of reporting debates 'inconvenient and unsatisfactory' and the reports themselves 'inadequate, their cost unnecessarily large and their publication unduly delayed', Hansards could not have been surprised to learn that their contract was to be terminated. The following year Thomas Hansard the second sold his business to a new public company, Hansard's Publishing Union, which proposed to report and print an independent account of the debates, asked for no subsidy and hoped to get advertising revenue. The company went bankrupt in 12 months however and the Stationery Office had to act quickly by giving the contract to a firm of outside printers. When in 1892 complaints were made once more of the inadequacy of the reports, another Select Committee met to consider the matter but failed to come up with any solution. So the Treasury tried the experiment of letting out the contract to report and print the debates to the lowest tender – and a series of printers lost money over it. When Arthur Balfour gave evidence to the next Select Committee which met to decide what to do in 1908 he said:

> I do not believe that these sketch accounts of what goes on within our walls, even if they are impartial (which they rarely or never are) are in any sense a substitute for reasoned argument.

The Committee thought the existing system entirely unsatisfactory whereby two-thirds of the speeches of Members were reported in the unofficial *Parliamentary Debates* in the third person, while ministers and ex-ministers were reported fully in the first person. It recommended that the House of Commons should have a reporting staff of its own and publish a full report of each speech 'which though not strictly verbatim is substantially the verbatim report, with repetitions and redundancies omitted and with obvious mistakes corrected, but which on the other hand leaves out nothing that adds to the meaning of the speech'. The proposals were adopted and came into force in 1909 with a staff of 11 reporters under the authority of a standing Publication and Reports Committee in consultation with the Speaker.

The 'hot air' which rose daily during sessions of Parliament happily disposed of itself, but someone had to remove the waste paper which accumulated in public offices – 10,000 tons of it between 1881 and 1887. Up to 1884 it had been sent to prisons where, because the Government insisted it should be made illegible, it was torn to shreds by convicts. But the Home Office thought this improper work for a prison population, and in 1885 the Stationery Office agreed to hire 52 girls to do the tearing for £1,200 a year. The freeing of paper from excise duty had lowered prices but sale of the shredded paper for pulping still brought £11,300 a year. It would have brought more, said Digby Pigott, if it had been sold as recovered from Whitehall wastepaper baskets, but security was overriding.

The most important step of all at this time, in the process of centralizing stationery and printing services in the hands of the Controller, came in 1889 when Queen Victoria granted him Royal Letters Patent appointing him 'Printer to Her Majesty of all Acts of Parliament' though, as seen, he contracted the work out. It was the end of the long private monopoly of the Printers to Her Majesty. Acts had to be sold at prices which the Treasury considered fair and reasonable.


## End of an era

In his third report of 1890, Digby Pigott gleefully reported that 'the cost of a first class battleship, complete with its armament, with an attendant flotilla of half-a-dozen gunboats, has during the last 10 years been saved, without inconvenience to the public, on Government printing and stationery'. For such an achievement was the Stationery Office created, and it was something of which he could be justifiably proud. But maybe it made him over-confident. That same year the Public Accounts Committee told him that he could give contractors advances on their payments of not more than five-sixths of the total bill at his discretion 'in special cases'. But in 1893, when he had been Controller for 15 years, they examined his books and felt he had overstepped the mark when in several instances he had given them more than five-sixths. When challenged on this, Digby Pigott said such arrangements were both regular and advantageous to the public service, but admitted not getting Treasury sanction. He had done it as a favour to contractors to meet immediate and pressing liabilities. 'Ready-money payments' tended to lower prices. But he was not allowed to get away with it. In future, said the Committee, all forms of contract used by the Stationery Office must be approved by the Treasury.

Digby Pigott survived this lapse with his usual aplomb. The Liberals were back in power under Gladstone who recognized the value of the role now being played by Her Majesty's Stationery Office by giving its head a knighthood – which no one had ever thought of giving the popular John McCulloch. It was not only recognition but appreciation. For the hard-worked, apparently indispensable Sir Thomas, who suffered frequent long spells of illness, it was a great honour.

The civil servant was not generally regarded as hard-working. J.B. Gotts, who rose to be Establishment Officer and Assistant Controller of the Stationery Office, reported to Storey's Gate on 15 March 1898 to take up his appointment as a technical printing clerk dressed – or over-dressed ? – in a new frock coat and glossy silk hat. He was on a salary of £100 a year which, if he stayed the course for 12 years, would become £250. He had no alternative but to conform to the prescribed office hours but he was dismayed by the general air of inertia. He considered civil servants a lazy lot who, like the fountains in Trafalgar Square, played from ten to four.

During Sir Thomas's absences, responsibility for running the Stationery Office fell to Mr Plowman, the Assistant Controller, who would have been more aware than his boss of the arrival in February 1899 of a newcomer of the lowest grade to Storey's Gate – Edward Chapman. Seventy years later that clerk recalled how Plowman would never allow anyone to give fog as an excuse for late attendance, and would frequently stand outside the front door five minutes before leaving time, with his pocket watch in his hand, to greet early leavers with a sarcastic reference to the punctuality of their departure.

That first day was not the ordeal he had expected:

> A building of some architectural pretensions fronted with a sickly privet hedge loomed before my eyes; through massive iron entrance gates lay a granite cobbled square backed by a warehouse and centred by a horse trough at which a thirsty beast was nuzzling to its content. Entering by the rising steps, after being genially challenged by Searle, the Metropolitan Police Sergeant in command of the portal, I was ushered up to the registry on the first floor. Here, where all outside was cold and gloom, inside was glowing warmth from a huge coal fire and a small staff as affable as the Cherryble Brothers.

Edward Chapman's job as a clerk in the Accounts Branch earned him £70 a year with £5 annual increments. On taking his seat that first day a gaunt elderly man in a black skull cap, Office Keeper Wilson, gave him a towel and half a cake of Letour's 'Windsor' Soap with the compliments of Time Keeper Plowman.

It was the beginning of a long career but, with the death of Queen Victoria, the end of an era for the country as well as for Her Majesty's Stationery Office.

# PART II

## 1901 – 1980

### Financial discipline
### Turn of century resentment

The Treasury has grown from being the guardian of the strong box to becoming the universal controller of every Department of HMG. It regards all other Departments as inferior to itself; it looks upon them as licentious spendthrifts, as prodigal sons from whose voracious maw it is the province of the Treasury to seize the fatted calf. The result is that all Departments labour under a more than Egyptian bondage.

MR GIBSON BOWLES
*MP for Lyme Regis, in Commons debate, 20 March 1900*

### End of century accord

We have for once – it is very rare that Governments actually do it – met unanimously and in full the recommendations of a report of the Expenditure Committee.

MR PAUL CHANNON
*MP, Minister of State, HM Treasury, in Commons debate on HMSO Trading Fund Order, 24 March 1980*

# CHAPTER 4

# Barometer of
# public service activity

## 1901 — 1921

*Selling books, distributing forms*

Symbolic of the new century and the new reign was the addition at Storey's Gate in 1902 of a telephone to the existing mechanical aids of 'three typewriters and one improved copying apparatus'. These new devices brought their problems. It was the impropriety of having one girl in an all-male staff which led to the initial purchase of two typewriters instead of one. As it was, the two girls were told to come to the office each day 15 minutes after everyone else and leave 15 minutes earlier. They were given keys for the Controller's WC, which they were free to use except on Monday and Saturday, the only two days on which the Controller put in an appearance. What arrangements were made for them on these occasions is not recorded. Anyone who wanted to see the lady typists operating these machines had to obtain a signed Registry chit to gain entrance to their room, and no dallying – the chit had to be returned *within minutes*. Similarly only a few people were allowed to use the telephone, and those only with the permission of the Registrar. The practice of writing notes and sending them by messenger continued for some years.

Sir Thomas was coming to the end of his term and in his fourth and final report to the Treasury (drawn up in 1895 but for some reason not submitted to Parliament in a revised form until 1904) he said he was more glad to be offering an explanation for the increase in expenditure of more than 50 per cent since his last report 14 years previously, 'as I shall in less than a year be surrendering the trust confided to me by your Lordships 27 years ago'. With efficiency and economy still the Controller's guiding stars, he was able to bow out of office with a 30-page document which recorded the growth of the demands made on the Stationery Office by customers, not only for the supply of printing and paper, but the 'tools of the trade' of the kind he presumed was proportioned to the work to be done. Whereas 5,400 bottles of gum had been issued in 1884, some 19,300 were asked for in 1903; the 4,300 lb of pins of 1884 were now 11,300 lb; 93,000 dozen pencils had been ordered in 1903 whereas only 38,000 in 1884. In the 20 years the call on cord and thread, web and leather straps had doubled.

Savings had been made by the decision of 1897 to by-pass the middleman and order all paper for the public service direct from manufacturers; but the free distribution of *Debates* to MPs on demand from 1899 had added to Stationery Office expenditure. To handle the extra work the staff at Storey's Gate had been enlarged and so the cost. The 153 of 1884 (49 established officers and 104 temporaries) had become 300.

In 20 years the cost of printing, stationery and the rest for the Home, Foreign, Colonial and War Offices, for the Admiralty, Post Office, Board of Trade, Patent Office and Board of Education had advanced by more than 90 per cent from £247,700 to £475,000. It was not infrequently urged that with a stronger hand at the Stationery Office the growth of expenditure might be kept under control. The Department, if it did its duty, could always ensure that prices were not excessive, 'but with regard to printing, the limits of its powers of useful interference are very soon reached'.

It was a plaint repeated by his successor Rowland Bailey of the Office of Works, who took over in 1905. He appealed to the compilers of the reports of Royal Commissions to curtail the printing of so much evidence, so many maps and diagrams, such wordy appendices. Everything not in the report was thrown into an appendix – 'a sort of waste-paper basket of the Commission':

> The only control at present exercised over the amount of matter published by Departments and Commissions is that of the Treasury. This control is insufficient because the Treasury has no absolute power to forbid an expenditure which another Department considers necessary. In

practice each Department orders what printing it chooses, gives away
gratuitously as many copies of each of its own publications as it cares to
do, and charges the whole cost upon the Estimates of the Stationery
Office.

The Select Committee of 1906 which came to that conclusion
recommended a Sessional Parliamentary Committee to which the
Controller might refer cases where matter was needlessly printed,
and assist the Speaker to supervise House of Commons printing.
Once again, the politicians recommended creating a Government
Printing Department 'sufficiently extensive for confidential and
urgent work', but once again the Treasury turned the idea down
as it did in 1909 for a Post Office Press, as it did in 1914 for 'a
small State Printing Office'. But in 1907 the Controller did
become printer and publisher of the *Votes and Proceedings* and
*Journals* of the House of Commons; and in 1909 publisher of
*Hansard* which then changed from an authorized, but unofficial
condensed report delivered six days after the events it reported to
an official verbatim report delivered to all Members of Parliament
the next morning.

The Controller had become the Queen's Printer of Acts of
Parliament in Scotland in 1901, and in March five years later a
Stationery Office was opened in Edinburgh with three clerical
and technical members and two warehousemen. Its creation was
the result of the administrative changes which followed the
passing of the Secretary for Scotland Act of 1885 which
transferred to the new Minister a list of duties previously carried
out under various statutory powers by the Home Secretary, the
Privy Council, the Treasury and the Local Government Board.

When the contract with the authorized Stationery Office
bookselling agent in Edinburgh, Oliver and Boyd, expired in
1911, the Treasury agreed to an experiment of direct selling.
Thus in 1912 Edinburgh became the location of the first
Government sale office. It had a staff of three booksellers. The
work of the Stationery Office in Edinburgh expanded as a result
of the social legislation of 1908 to 1911 and then, during the Great
War, additional staff and accommodation were needed to meet
the demands of troops stationed in Scotland and of the various
large munitions factories in the area.

The Stationery Office's Irish agency also lapsed in 1911, but the Treasury insisted on finishing the two-year trial in Edinburgh, to which it had agreed very reluctantly, before considering a sale office in Dublin.

Arranging for the distribution of Government books at sale offices was very much less complicated than distributing the flood of forms needed to operate the Old Age Pensions Act of 1908 and other legislation of Lloyd George's People's Budget. Hitherto the Stationery Office had only delivered printed items in bulk to Government Departments, but they were now required to distribute a variety of pension forms to some 1,400 local committees. The National Insurance Act of 1911 meant having to deliver 50 million membership cards and other forms to 20,000 addresses. For the distribution of forms on this scale they acquired a sausage and meat factory in Shepherdess Walk in North London, where they installed mechanical addressing and warehousing equipment. It was known to Stationery Office staff as 'the Ice Well'.

The Old Age Pensions Act was only one of many increasing burdens on the administrative work of Government Departments who were turning more and more to typewriters for correspondence. The rising cost of having these machines repaired by outside firms led the Stationery Office in 1910 to appoint its own mechanic, Claude Healy, at a wage of £2 10s a week. He made a great success of the job, and from it grew the Office Machinery Technical Service (OMTS) of the 1980s.

The meticulous planning for these operations was one of the last activities of Sir Rowland Bailey (knighthoods for Controllers were now customary) whom Edward Chapman described as 'energetic and impetuous'. He expected all to be on their toes and at their post when he rang for their attendance. When visiting other Government offices in London he invariably took with him Challis, the Head Messenger, travelling side by side in a hansom.

In 1913 Sir Rowland retired to Sheringham and handed over to Frederick Atterbury (later also knighted), 'a calm and deliberate man, the very antithesis of Sir Rowland, who adopted a canny way of saving himself unnecessary brain-work when promotions in the staff were on the tapis':

Having selected several files awaiting his decision in which there was conflict between the executive and the technical sides, he would have each recommended candidate in his own room and set him to give what would have been his decision, with added reasons why. Whether this wheeze worked is not for me to say but at least it added to Sir Frederick's reputation for shrewdness.

## War changes the load

The South African War placed little strain on the resources of the Stationery Office, but the very different nature of the Great War which broke out in 1914 demanded all the shrewdness its Controller could muster, and the quick reaction of all staff to the unprecedented problems which the emergency presented.

For Sir Frederick it began three days *before* the British Government declared war:

Shortly before midnight on Saturday 1 August 1914 I was asked by the Treasury whether I could arrange for an issue of one-pound Treasury notes within a week of that date.

The Mint had coined gold sovereigns and half-sovereigns since time immemorial, but they now had to be withdrawn from circulation to help pay the cost of waging war. No British Government had had occasion to print money (except for 14 years between 1797 and 1811) until the man from the Inland Revenue (the department of the Treasury given the responsibility for their manufacture) bearded the Controller at home that sad weekend when the lights were going out all over Europe. It called for quick thinking, and Atterbury told his visitor the job could certainly be done so long as he could lay hands on sufficient stocks of suitable paper. By 'suitable' he meant uncounterfeitable. What about the paper used for penny stamps? The pound notes could be printed on that to give a temporary measure of security – there is no linen fibre in stamp paper – and the first issue could be replaced as soon as possible by one of a more elaborate design and character.

The legend is that Sir Frederick Atterbury drew out a rough sketch for Britain's first one-pound note on a pad of writing paper there and then in his drawing room. The work was given to Waterlow Brothers and Layton Limited who had a professionally drawn design, and the wording, completed by Monday, and the plates ready by Tuesday. The main difficulty was to be consecutive numbering, which the resourceful Waterlows solved by buying up all the available numbering barrels in the UK.

The following version of what occurred is given in *The House of Waterlow Under Six Reigns*:

> When the Treasury and the bankers realised that war was inevitable – and that was two days before this country declared itself hostile to Germany and her allies – it was recognised that a new currency was necessary, and that the seemingly impossible must be achieved. At this critical period Waterlows were consulted by His Majesty's Stationery Office on behalf of the Treasury, and confronted with a proposition of such magnitude that the management might well have recoiled from undertaking its execution. Fortunately, both the management and the staff had the appetite and capacity for the task.
>
> The first order was for four million treasury notes. Instructions were given on the afternoon of Sunday August 2nd, 1914 and, by the morning of August 7th when the banks re-opened, these four million £1 notes were in the hands of the bankers! The design had to be prepared, the plates made, the notes printed, numbered and distributed to the bankers . . . This is not the end of the story: the Treasury were satisfied, and the firm continued to deliver five million notes a day for several days.

The order for ten-shilling notes was given to Messrs De La Rue. On 5 August they received a letter from the Stationery Office requesting them to make the notes with paper which would be supplied by Inland Revenue. 'All the processes to be under strict control. The output as regards number to be to the satisfaction of the Treasury.' In the offices of Thomas De La Rue in 1984 was a framed proof of this first ten-shilling note on which was written in ink:

Plate approved   F. Atterbury 7/8/14

Underneath the signed proof, the firm told the story of how it came to be printed:

> The design of necessity was very hurriedly composed, but so successful were we in reorganising our factories that we were able to produce the

proof shown in black on August 6th, which was approved the following day. On August 17th particulars were given to us by the Secretary of the Inland Revenue with a request for the preparation of designs of a £1 currency note. One was chosen following exactly the 10/- subsequently ordered, of which a specimen is shewn, except that the size was larger. A proof was approved in black as a colour standard on October 1st, 1914. As an example of the urgency of producing these notes at the earliest possible moment, we would mention that the Factory and Workshop Act of 1901 was amended on August 19th by the Secretary of State for Home Affairs to permit us to employ women on a system of eight hour shifts 24 hours a day whilst working on these currency notes.

So just how the first one-pound treasury note of 1914 came to be designed and printed seems to be a matter of debate. But it is common knowledge how they came to be called 'Bradburys'. Many thought it was because they had been printed by the security printer Bradbury Wilkinson, but it was in fact because they had been signed prominently by John Bradbury, Secretary to the Treasury. The similarity of the names was a coincidence.

Soon Atterbury was being asked to organize the printing of war savings certificates, but he was given a little more time for that. The demand for manuals such as *Infantry Training* rocketed from 20,000 a year to 500,000. Requests came in at a rate of 200 a day for manuals and stationery from small army units all over Britain. The print run of some publications was astronomical: a million copies each of Sir Edward Grey's White Paper on the events leading up to the outbreak of war, and Lord Bryce's on German outrages. From everywhere came requisitions for typewriters, slide rules and adding machines, for cash registers, tabulating machines and rotary duplicators.

Having so often rejected the idea of the Stationery Office undertaking its own printing, the war forced the hand of the Treasury when in November 1916 Messrs Darling and Son, who held a large number of Stationery Office contracts for printing, indicated that this work was no longer profitable. Only an annual 'allowance' of £3,000 a year, they said, would enable them to complete their contracts and prevent them closing down. The Stationery Office refused to subsidize them but offered to take over their Press in Hare Street, London, for as long as the war lasted and six months afterwards. Their directors agreed, and on

26 February 1917 handed over the entire management of the works to the Stationery Office. In May 1920 the Stationery Office bought the plant outright for £20,000.

The next acquisition arose from a request by the Admiralty for better and increased facilities for their Confidential printing. For this a Press was taken over in November 1917 in Dugdale Street, Bethnal Green, again for the period of the war and six months after. The third wartime take-over was in March 1918 when compulsory powers were taken under the Defence of the Realm Act (DORA) to meet the large and urgent requirements of the Ministry of Food. The firm chosen was Messrs Hayman, Christy and Lilly Ltd in Farringdon Road, whose workshops were rented and plant purchased. But they were unable to handle the rush order from the Ministry of Food for 78 million ration books. For this the Government requisitioned the works of David Allen & Company in Harrow after consulting their competitors Waterlow Brothers, who were then commissioned to print the non-forgeable coupons at high speed – each five-page book necessitating 12 printings – an operation in which they were highly experienced. A duplicating and distributing unit was created to handle the millions of facsimile letters of appeal for war charities signed by Queen Mary, the Prince of Wales and Princess Mary. Most of the plant, machinery and staff of the Dugdale Street works and of the Farringdon Road works were transferred to Harrow when both these were given up in March 1921.

War also forced Government Departments to curb expenditure on print and stationery in a way no peacetime pleading had ever done. A 1915 Commons Committee suggested that all Departments curtailed annual reports of work which in time of peace would have influenced public policy but would now pass with little notice; and this was done, often drastically. The Board of Education compressed their normal 3,167 pages a year into 663. Departments responded in the 'new spirit of war economy' to Atterbury's catalogue of Parliamentary Papers, from which he invited them to order only the individual papers they wanted, rather than a whole class as was their wont. Retrenchment was once more the order of the day at home, and no small part of the spur to act on it was a realization of the very much greater sacrifices being made by those no longer at home, fighting the enemy in the mud of Flanders.

However, the war did not prevent changes in arrangements for selling Government publications. In 1915 the Edinburgh experiment was officially deemed a success and the sale of Government publications throughout the UK was formally entrusted to the Stationery Office. The contract with agents Wyman was terminated at the end of 1916, and the following year new sale offices for Government publications were opened in Cardiff, Manchester (where a branch office and depot had already been opened in Peter Street) and London in Kingsway and Abingdon Street (closed in 1926).

As William Cox, later to retire as Deputy Controller, had to admit, these early sale offices (not 'bookshops' till 1954) were far from attractive. 'The window displays were drab and the interiors were little more than extensions of the publications warehouse, with hundreds of dusty pigeon-holes filled with bundles untidily labelled by hand.' But the change to direct selling was a success from the start.

### Behind the lines in France; branching out in Britain

Frederick Atterbury went to see the six Army Printing and Stationery depots operating in France in 1915 and found that some 400 men were making an efficient job of this important, non-combatant exercise under 17 officers. When his Superintendent of Demands William Codling went out two years later, the Army Printing and Stationery Service (APSS) had 13 stations run by 850 men under 52 officers. Being of a confidential nature, said Codling in his report to Atterbury, the work ought not to be entrusted to local French firms. Because it was all urgent 'it was a supreme advantage to the military authorities to be able to obtain it in France'. Women were helping with printing and warehouse work. It must have surprised Atterbury to be told that 'the work being done under war conditions in the field was, if anything, better than in the Stationery Office. The army stationery services have the advantage of military discipline which is of course conducive to this end'. The Photographic Sections excited his unbounded admiration by supplying ground troops with prints of aerial photographs taken by the Royal Flying Corps. There was a well-organized system for the issue and repair of typewriters.

During the Great War some 22,000 typewriters were purchased, making the number in service when it ended about 30,000. A travelling inspector was appointed to ensure that machines not in use were returned for repair and re-issue. He did the job so well that no new typewriters were bought for another six years.

Codling made another visit to France in October 1918 accompanied by Captain Stenson Cooke, head of the newly created Stationery Office Inspectorate Department and Secretary of the Automobile Association (a post he managed to combine with his military duties). The small unit of three officers and seven men who had gone out in August 1914 with the British Expeditionary Force to issue army forms, books and stationery had grown to 1,000 other ranks and 65 officers in France and Belgium alone, apart from other theatres of war such as Italy, Egypt, Salonika and Mesopotamia. There was now a Director of the APSS at GHQ who had absolute control of Stationery Office Votes overseas. The new Royal Air Force had its own Printing and Stationery Service. It was probably on this occasion that Codling met Norman Scorgie who, having joined the Army in 1915 as a subaltern after a distinguished career at Cambridge, was by 1918 a Lieutenant-Colonel and Deputy Director of the APSS. Subsequent events were to show how great an impression Codling gained of him.

At home it became necessary to divide England into two, and establish a Northern Area Branch (NAB) based on Manchester. To the administrative office opened at 37 Peter Street in June 1916 were soon added a forms depot in Salford, two paper depots in Oldham, another at nearby Further Hey Mill and the extensive American Aircraft Acceptance Park at Failsworth (Chadderton), built for the assembly of Handley Page bombers made in America. Some 540 staff worked for the Stationery Office in Manchester between 1916 and 1918, issued 1,143,000,000 forms in 62,000 varieties and, if there had been the demand, they could have issued 678,000 Bibles and prayer books to the fighting forces.

The establishment of NAB to serve England north of a line from the Severn to the Wash, and Wales, avoided an extension of the London-based Inland Revenue store at Somerset House, the Customs and Excise store at Old Jewry and the Post Office store at Studd Street, and enabled the Board of Trade to give up two buildings at Poplar. For William Cox, NAB 'had practically everything that London had to offer' – printing and binding, forms store, a big warehouse and a very well run canteen. There were grass plots where games were played in the dinner hour until a bell was rung five minutes before the break ended, and a 'playable' crown bowling green. It even boasted a lady welfare officer which was unusual for those times, and (more in period) an amateur dramatic society whose standards are unrecorded but were probably no less high than those of London's Stationery Office Singers of the same period, who attained such high levels of performance when revived by Roland Owen in the 1960s.

The needs of Scotland were catered for by Edinburgh Branch, which was smaller than Manchester and also had no printing works. All printing ordered had to be done on a contractual print procurement basis. There was always pressure that the paper they used should be ordered through Scottish mills. The branch supplied all Scottish Departments, which were mainly in the capital, and all sheriffs and procurators fiscal throughout Scotland. Apart from the sale office, there was a warehouse and an Office Machine Repair Section opened around 1921.

The staff, as elsewhere in the Civil Service between the wars, were required to work on Saturday mornings, but one day in the 1920s a memorandum arrived from the Scottish Office telling them that, though suits must be worn in the week, as a concession to golfers, anyone who wanted to could wear plus-fours. Looking back on his time at Edinburgh in those days William Cox said:

> My job in Edinburgh did show me the importance which was attached to the Stationery Office spreading its services over the whole country and

ensuring that the commercial interests of printing and supplies should
come as far as possible from the various regions.

A sizable duplicating section was opened there later. The
method of taking copies of letters had changed out of all
recognition since the days when letters typed with a 'copying
ribbon' were placed in copying books and put in a copying press,
the pressure from which, plus the damp tissue, produced a copy
for filing. It was then that a typewriter mechanic was easily
spotted by the purple marks he had on his hands and face, which
came from the dye on the copying ribbons. Spirit duplicating was
an innovation, but the real revolution did not come until 1928
with the introduction of offset-litho machines.

In London, Cornwall House, a very strong reinforced-concrete
building, had been built as a stationery and forms warehouse in
Stamford Street in South East London, to serve the Southern
Area. But before it could be used for this purpose it was
requisitioned in 1918 as the King George V Hospital for
Returning Soldiers. A memorial plaque outside the church in
Waterloo Road records those who died in Cornwall House as a
result of the wounds they received in the Great War. The
Stationery Office was not able to move into the new building until
1919.

### Serving the peacemakers

Ordinary annual estimates for the Stationery Office were now
running at more than £1 million, but the extraordinary demands
of war had added another £4 million. Total staff in 1918 was
1,355 men and 1,287 women. Sir Frederick Atterbury fell ill that
year, and though he had laid the plans for the services which the
Stationery Office had to provide for the Versailles Peace
Conference, he had to leave it to William Codling to carry them
out. When Atterbury was forced to resign from ill health, there
was a brief interregnum with Ulick Wintour as Controller before
the Treasury appointed as head of the Stationery Office someone,
as Edward Chapman put it, 'hatched from within'.

William Codling, the one-time Superintendent of Demands and now Assistant Controller, who had come to Storey's Gate as a 19-year-old junior clerk in 1898, became the first Controller – and so far the last – to have risen from the bottom of the hierarchy. One of his first actions in 1919 was to recruit Lieutenant-Colonel Scorgie as Deputy Controller at the age of 35. There was fury amongst the senior Stationery Office men – the Deputy post had until then always been filled from within – and they caused the appointment to be questioned in the House of Commons. But Stanley Baldwin, then Secretary to the Treasury, resolutely maintained that Colonel Scorgie 'was considered better qualified than any officer serving in the Stationery Office'. The following two decades were to provide many opportunities for Scorgie to demonstrate his high administrative ability and the wisdom of Codling's choice.

Enquiry had shown that it was going to be impossible to employ French workmen for the Peace Conference exercise. Preparations had to be made without knowing where the delegates were going to meet. Paper was bought and staff earmarked. Special presses were ordered earlier and stored in London, but after an air-raid were moved to Manchester. When the conference site was known the Linotype machines, the presses, the cases of type and the formes were taken out of storage, packed on a special train to Southampton and shipped across to Le Havre. A team from Storey's Gate journeyed to Versailles, found a site outside the fortifications, erected its own printing establishment and arranged accommodation for its staff. All was ready by January 1919. Once the sessions began, the Stationery Office supplied Lloyd George and his colleagues with daily printed verbatim reports of proceedings just like *Hansard*.

When the Foreign Office wanted printed matter at short notice in connection with a conference at home, it had the work done in the Press in the basement of its Whitehall building by Harrison & Sons. The running of this Press and its staff of 100 was taken over by the Stationery Office in November 1918. It carried out classified work up to the highest category (above 'Top Secret') not only for the Foreign Office but also for the Cabinet Office, Treasury and other Departments. Apart from its printing activities the Foreign Office Press provided a convenient 'packing station' for items which the FO post room could not deal with. Top hats, swords, regalia, bottles of medicine, and probably other liquids, were among the variety of ill-shaped items which the Press had to parcel up for dispatch to British embassies abroad.

The India Office Press, managed by Eyre & Spottiswoode, was taken over by the Stationery Office in October 1919 (and closed in 1938), and the War Office Press, managed by Harrison & Sons, in 1922 (closed in 1961). From 1918 it fell to the Stationery Office to arrange for the printing of the Lists and Registers of Electors of the whole of the UK which had previously been done by local authorities. The cost of it all in 1921 was £5 million (compared with £1.2 million in 1913). When the lithographic printing of weather reports and charts by contractors on Government premises in South Kensington was transferred to the Air Ministry in Kingsway in January 1920, the Press and its staff came under the control of the Stationery Office.

Not only the work but the problems built up. The old one of the Government not being seen to be competing with commercial interests came round once again in the guise of advertising. Publications like the *Army and Navy List* and *Post Office Guide* had taken advertisements from the 1850s. *The Times* had opposed the 'new departure' when the Stationery Office proposed having advertisements in the *Board of Trade Journal* in 1887, and the Newspaper Society had sent a deputation to protest at the Government putting itself into competition with private undertakings in 1892 and again in 1895. In 1917 a Government Advertising Advisory Committee was set up, and in spite of the objections, the policy of accepting advertisements in Government publications was widened in 1921.

To criticism of the Stationery Office on this score was added a general dissatisfaction with its pace. None was more aware of this than its Controller William Codling who, in an attempt to remove delays in clearing work, issued a series of internal notices (no doubt drafted by Scorgie) headed 'Do It Now'. Delay, he said, was a source of irritation to the general public on whose goodwill their salaries and positions ultimately depended. When a matter considered 'not urgent' took five weeks to report on, the public would think they had spent five weeks inventing an obstructive reply. If it had been a favourable one, all the grace would have gone out of it by the delay. Anyone who day after day sat and gazed on a pile of papers which an hour's solid work would dispose of was drugging his soul.

# CHAPTER 5

# From one peace towards another

## 1922 – 1942

*The best of a difficult situation*

Wartime expansion had put great strain on the Department's organization and shown the need for changes to meet the demands of the 20th century. In 1921 it was reshaped on lines which remained substantially unaltered for half a century. The post of Registrar was created to centralize the responsibility for official papers, and of Establishment Officer to look after staff (who in army fashion were called Personnel), office equipment and organization, accommodation and relations with contractors. A new Director of Supplies co-ordinated the work of purchasing, storing and issuing customers' requirements, and the repair of typewriters. There was a Director of Printing and Binding; a Chief Receiver and Examiner; a Director of Publications; a Superintendent of the Duplicating and Distributing Branch; a Director of Transport and a Director of Accounts. The post of Assistant Controller was abolished and his duties re-distributed.

Stationery Office interest in election work began with the supply and distribution of stamping instruments to Returning Officers in 1922. By 1924 it held sufficient stocks to supply them with both perforating instruments to replace those for stamping, and election stationery and forms. They had to be supplied to Returning Officers within three weeks of an Election Writ being issued. Enough were kept to repeat the operation in the event of the election not leading to the formation of a new Government, and another general election having to be held immediately.

In 1924 Supplies Directorate were asked to supply items of office machinery and stationery to the Foreign Office for the Dawes Conference called to report on the issue of reparations from defeated Germany. From this sprang the Division's Conference Service which also dealt with demands from the Royal Household. At all the national and international conferences for which its services were required, Supplies Division organized machine maintenance, and made sure they could meet any unforeseen circumstance.

The new Publications Division was charged with:

> the work of publishing, the necessary and attendant publicity, the preservation of Crown Copyright, the supply of Government publications to Government Departments, to the wholesale and retail bookselling trade and to the general public . . .

In 1921 there was a small section to deal with cataloguing and publicity which was responsible also for the selection and appointment of agents at home and overseas, and for liaison and stimulation of bookshop activities. The first commissioned representative was employed in 1922 but the experiment was discontinued after five years as being uneconomic. A start was made on building up a network of bookshop agents in the provinces and overseas.

From 1900 to 1921 separate quarterly lists for Parliamentary and non-Parliamentary publications were issued and each was consolidated annually. From 1922 they were both combined in one volume. Daily publishing lists of Parliamentary and non-Parliamentary publications were introduced in 1922 to improve the flow of information to the public, and particularly bookshops and libraries. Keeping up to date by monthly, quarterly or even six-monthly consolidations presented considerable problems however.

The Stationery Office was not left alone to get on with its business. The Labour Government of 1924 pressed for cheaper Blue Books in order to have their policies understood by the poorer sections of the community; but in 1925, on a change of Government, the prices of some publications were increased by up to 200 per cent to recover their costs. Critics of the overall drabness of Stationery Office publications were never lacking; in response, a Type Faces Committee reported in 1922 and significant improvements resulted in typography and paper. A re-design of the Royal Arms followed in 1924. In 1925 a 'Printing Officer' was appointed to re-design title pages – the genesis of Stationery Office concern with graphic design.

In that year some 113 Parliamentary Questions, mainly querying the Stationery Office's role as publisher *and* bookseller and alleging its ineptitude in both, were put down for answer in the Commons. When Cornwall House ceased being King George's Hospital and later, in 1922, the wholesale stocks of Government publications were moved to this building south of the Thames, the newspapers protested that it was too far from Fleet Street. Shortage of labour at home during the war had made trade unions stronger, and in 1923 the *London Gazette* failed to appear for the first time in 258 years because of a strike at the printers, Wymans. The Stationery Office then transferred the printing to its own Press in Hare Street.

Reorganization in Britain coincided with revolution in Ireland. With the passing of the Government of Ireland Act 1920, by which a separate administration was set up for Ulster, a need arose to provide for the new Northern Ireland Government's printing and stationery, and a Stationery Office branch was opened in Belfast. Up to 1921 the Stationery Office had served the Six Counties through its Dublin branch, and the Belfast Office was created as a matter of convenience during the transfer of power to the North. Although the Government of Northern Ireland had the option to run the Belfast Office itself, it chose to perpetuate the interim arrangement whereby the Stationery Office provided the necessary printing and stationery services, including the production of a *Belfast Gazette*.

Additional responsibility of another kind came the way of the Stationery Office at this time when it was asked by the Admiralty to undertake the production of charts, which their Lordships however would continue to store and distribute. For this the Office of Works acquired premises at Cricklewood, formerly occupied by the Sunbeam Company, which became the Admiralty Chart Establishment in April 1923. It remained under the

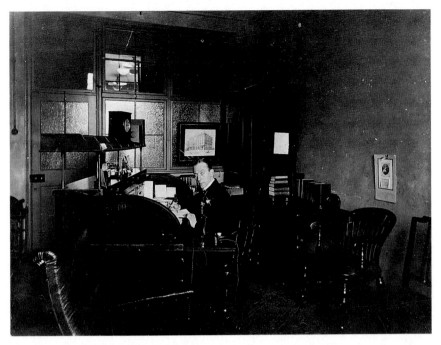

14. Edward Chapman joined the Stationery Office at Storey's Gate as a £70 a year clerk in 1899 and enjoyed a successful career (he is seen here in his office in Manchester). His reminiscences provide a colourful picture of life in the Stationery Office at the turn of the century.

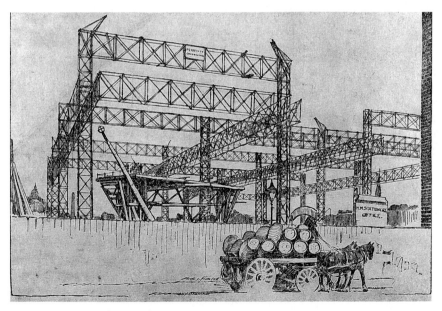

15. The construction of Cornwall House, close by Waterloo Station, as a warehouse for Government publications aroused a lot of interest when begun just before the Great War. It was the first substantial building in London to use reinforced concrete.

16. The Great War drove Britain off the gold standard and paper currency had to be prepared hurriedly. It is believed that the Stationery Office Controller, Sir Frederick Atterbury, sketched the designs in his drawing-room.

17. The Stationery Office Northern Area Branch established at Failsworth, Manchester, in 1916.

18. The Composing Room in the first Stationery Office Press at Farringdon Road, London, in 1920.

19. The busy Duplicating Section at Shepherdess Walk in the years immediately following the end of the Great War.

20. A London *Evening News* cartoon of April 1926 commenting on a four-volume treatise issued by the Stationery Office on economy in the use of official stationery.

# The British Gazette

Published by His Majesty's Stationery Office.

No. 1.      LONDON, WEDNESDAY, MAY 5, 1926.      ONE PENNY.

## FIRST DAY OF GREAT STRIKE

### Not So Complete as Hoped by its Promoters

### PREMIER'S AUDIENCE OF THE KING

#### Miners and the General Council Meet at House of Commons

---

## FOOD SUPPLIES

### No Hoarding: A Fair Share for Everybody

### MILK DISTRIBUTION

#### Control or Supplies in the Metropolis

### LAW COURTS AT WORK

#### Judge on the Duty of the Public

### G.P.O. SERVICES

#### Restrictions on Telegrams and Letters

### THE KING RECEIVES THE PREMIER

---

## HOLD-UP OF THE NATION

### Government and the Challenge

### NO FLINCHING

#### The Constitution or a Soviet

---

## COMMUNIST LEADER ARRESTED

### Mr. Saklatvala, M.P., Charged at Bow Street

### SEQUEL TO MAY DAY SPEECH

#### GOVERNMENT'S VIEW

#### SPECIAL CONSTABLES

Appeal to Capable Citizens in London to Enrol

#### THE CHOICE

#### RESERVE OF OFFICERS

---

## THE "BRITISH GAZETTE" AND ITS OBJECTS

### Reply to Strike Makers' Plan to Paralyse Public Opinion

### REAL MEANING OF THE STRIKE

#### Conflict Between Trade Union Leaders and Parliament

#### NO ADVANCE ON JULY

#### NO SECTIONAL DICTATION

#### DANGER OF RUMOURS

#### PROSPERITY AT STAKE

---

21. The two-page daily bulletin which the Stationery Office published for the Government during the General Strike of 1926 was called the *British Gazette*.

22. The Stationery Office began printing telephone directories at Harrow Press (above) in 1922.

23. 'Wireless' was among the subjects on which customers could buy Government publications at the public counter of the Manchester Sale Office in 1927. Others were in London, Edinburgh and Cardiff at this time.

# GOSSIP of SOUTH WALES

### Conducted By "The STROLLER"

I NOTE that despite the public agitation that has been made about the matter, the right of way to the Ystradfellte Caves is still being challenged by the farmer concerned.

When the question of charging a fee to gain access to the caves was first raised, I went there and discovered that 2d. per person was being charged.

Last Sunday I went again, and found that I had to pay 3d., an increase of 50 per cent., and on top of that I had to pay another 3d. because I had to leave my small car in an adjoining field because I could not take it to the cave with me, or leave it on the road, which was too narrow to permit two cars to pass.

The argument advanced by farmers in the neighbourhood at the Penderyn Council some time ago was that the farmer had to make a charge in order to preserve his rights and protect himself against people who damaged his property.

❋ ❋ ❋

### Deprived Pleasure

That was a reasonable argument, but if fees are going to be increased at the same rate as they have been during the past 12 months, then it is going to mean that hundreds of ordinary folk, school children and young people who make pilgrimages to Ystradfellte during the summer will be deprived of a pleasure and a right that has been undisputed for hundreds of years.

If some attempt had been made to aid sightseers, the matter would not be so open to criticism. In some famous English caves a guide is provided and conducts parties through the dangerous passages. At the Ystradfellte Caves no one seems concerned about the safety of the public.

❋ ❋ ❋

### First in the Country

ALTHOUGH we in Wales may be saying nasty things about Government Departments because they will not bring R.A.F. schools, arsenals, and what not to Cardiff and the distressed areas, nobody seems to notice when one of them actually does break new ground in the city.

I see that H.M. Stationery Office in St. Andrew's-crescent have installed a cycle delivery box for the Government publications it handles. All you have to do is to ring up Cardiff 2254, tell the official in charge that you want card so and so, and almost before you have hung up the earpiece there will be a uniformed official at your door with the publication—and the bill.

**FIRST OF ITS KIND IN THE COUNTRY**

And what is more, Cardiff is the only city in the country where you can do it. The department is trying it on the Welsh dog.

❋ ❋ ❋

### Transport Board

CARDIFF Corporation Transport Band, which has done so well in the past, and which this year took a premier award and a second prize in the Crystal Palace competitions and followed that by a clear win in Class A. at Pontypridd, are hoping to do even better to-morrow, when they compete in the big May championships at Belle Vue, Manchester.

As at Crystal Palace, they will find themselves one of 26 bands entered in the Class A. competition, and all the famous bands of the North are against them. But that does not deter them, and when they leave with their conductor, Mr. D. Carrie, on Friday for Cottonopolis it will be with a feeling of optimism that after all the hard work they have put in the test piece, "Die Feen," it will have to be a strong band that will beat them.

They are playing extremely well just now, too, and they are enheartened by the fact that they have been invited to be one of the units building up the massed band of 2,500 performers that is to give a centenary performance at the close of the competitions. Anyhow, here's wishing them luck on Saturday.

❋ ❋ ❋

### Opportunity Knocks

FOR some months past, the drama and feature programme assistants at the Welsh Regional Station, Cardiff, have been searching for new actors who can make a success of the microphone technique. In a country so rich in histrionic ability as Wales, it would seem an easy task to discover large numbers of competent actors; but experience has proved that the task is by no means as easy as it looks.

There is a great demand for radio actors with real ability, and the dramatic assistants at Cardiff are out to find them. Actors who are interested in radio work should write to the Regional Director at Cardiff, requesting an audition.

When a sufficient number of requests have been received, the dramatic assistants will spend a few days at Cardiff, Swansea and Bangor, listening to prospective actors, and testing their suitability to the microphone. It is hoped that a considerable amount of new talent will be discovered in this way.

❋ ❋ ❋

### Just Titles

I HAVE been looking at a long list of books recommended for purchase for a South Wales library,

---

24. Delivery of Government publications by cycle provided a good gossip item for the *South Wales Echo* of 8 May 1936. The Cardiff Office introduced the idea, but there is no evidence that any of the other Sale Offices took it up.

25. Bristol Office had a lucky escape from destruction in the Second World War when bombs fell on the building immediately opposite; a photograph taken in 1945 shows part of the bombed site (lower left corner).

26. Sir John Simpson, Controller (left), tries his hand at bookselling.

27. Garter King of Arms chose these designs for the invitation cards which Her Majesty's Stationery Office printed for the coronation of Queen Elizabeth II in 1953. The decorative border on the largest card was by Joan Hassall, and the wording was drawn by S.B. Stead of the Stationery Office Layout Section.

28. The Government Publications Warehouse and Post and Trade Bookshop at Cornwall House.

29. Paper testing in the HMSO Laboratory at Cornwall House.

30. In 1947 the Stationery Office acquired the Palace of Industry, built at Wembley for the British Empire Exhibition of 1925, as a warehouse and office (above).

31. From Wembley paper was delivered by van to printers.

32. Binding telephone directories at Harrow Press in 1961.

33. The British Museum Bindery in the 1960s. Repairing valuable old books was the principal activity.

34. For many years the main bookshop in London was in Kingsway.

35. The Kingsway Bookshop was closed and moved to Holborn in 1966.

36. Collating sheets of National Savings stamps at Manor Farm Press.

37. Examples of the items printed during the 1950s at Manor Farm Press by the photogravure process.

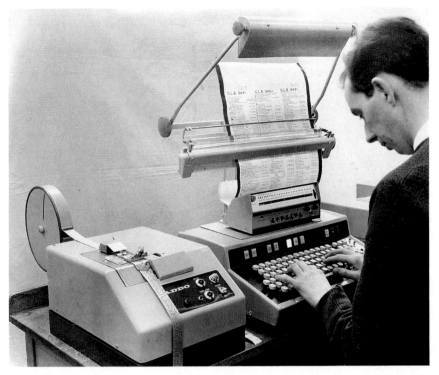

38. An early application of computer technology to typesetting was an Elliott 903B computer system in Edinburgh Press in 1965.

39. One of the high-speed telephone directory presses installed by HMSO at its Gateshead Press.

40. Atlantic House on Holborn Viaduct was one of the largest early post-war developments. It was the Stationery Office headquarters for more than a quarter of a century.

41. The choice of Norwich as the new out-of-London location of HMSO was announced in September 1964: Sovereign House in the final stages of construction in the summer of 1968.

management of the Stationery Office until March 1929 when the Admiralty took it back.

Customer Departments had so far never known what they spent on printing and stationery every year, and a Commons Committee of 1921 considered this 'detrimental to good management and economy in ordering'; but in 1924 the Treasury told the Speaker that to notify each Department of its expenditure was impractical. It would not, apparently, lead to either efficiency or economy. It was sufficient that the total State expenditure on printing was shown in the annual Stationery Office Vote. It had risen from £60,000 in 1825 to £5,300,000 in 1920 and dropped to £4,200,000 in 1922. Only 20 years before it had been £600,000. The 1923 Committee on National Expenditure observed that the increase in the total Vote over pre-war expenditure represented far more than the rise in prices and the normal growth of Departments.

### Responding to change

The Stationery Office did not make films, nor was its Controller interested in doing so, but in 1925 a man with the title 'Technical Adviser on Cinematography to HM Government' was put on the payroll of the Stationery Office without actually being a member of its staff. Edward Foxen-Cooper was an authority on film storage and the custodian of the official films of the Great War. His activities had come to light through the filming of the signing of the Locarno Treaty at the Foreign Office in December 1925. As the Controller of the Stationery Office was by Letters Patent the holder of Crown Copyright, it was not unreasonable for Foxen-Cooper to be given official status by attachment to the Stationery Office, which from then on became responsible for copyright control of any film produced for the Government service. It took over custody of the Imperial War Museum films, gave advice on the storage and preservation of all Government films, helped Departments with the contracts they made for film production, and even provided facilities for seeing them in the Stationery Office theatre in the basement of the War Office in

Whitehall. Some 600 tins containing 600,000 feet of film about
the Great War were stored at, and issued from, Northern Area
Branch at Manchester. Responsibility for the Government
Cinematograph Adviser, as he came to be called, was to remain
with the Stationery Office until the 1950s, when it was
transferred to the Central Office of Information.

The Stationery Office however was much more concerned with
putting words on paper than pictures on celluloid. All Government printing works were union houses up to the ten-day General
Strike of 1926, when 619 out of 715 at Harrow joined in, 65 out of
85 at the Foreign Office Press and 23 out of 24 at the War Office
Press. Non-unionists were engaged to take their place, and at the
end of the strike the Stationery Office adopted an open-house
policy, with freedom to employ unionists or non-unionists. This
was modified in 1929 when all *new* staff had to be unionists.
During the emergency Winston Churchill published a daily
Government bulletin which he wanted to call the *London Gazette*
to give it the official prestige of that publication. But, Norman
Scorgie recalled, 'Codling and I fought determinedly against
losing the identity of the *London Gazette* for a passing advantage,
and the *British Gazette* was created for the duration of the strike'.
The manufacture of paper stopped, and existing stocks were
insufficient for the big print issue of the daily *British Gazette*. So
Bowaters' mill at Northfleet was commandeered and Stationery
Office laboratory staff volunteered to help make the paper
without which the Government's General Strike news-sheet
would never have gone on the streets. Both they and the
Bowaters' employees who agreed to lend a hand were subjected
to considerable intimidation, which was called off on the
appearance of 60 uniformed infantrymen with rifles at the ready.

A general strike apart, there were always those who took every
opportunity to oppose the concept of State printing and they were
successful in having another Treasury Committee (chaired by
Colonel J. Gretton MP) investigate it from all angles. After four
years (in 1927) the Committee produced an exhaustive review of
the pros and cons but advocated no change. The Gretton
Committee Report was a milestone for the Stationery Office
however. It validated the principle of State-owned printing works

for executing work of a confidential or very urgent nature, or of a specialized type. At that time about one third of all the printing ordered from the Stationery Office was produced in its factories, and the Committee thought this reasonable. Their observation was for many later years treated as an absolute rule, and consequently had significant effect on the development of printing and, later, binding resources by the Stationery Office.

For Codling, the head of a supply service which was still merely an agent of Treasury control, the findings of such time-consuming investigations, however favourable, rarely made his job easier. As one informed observer, W.R. Barker, wrote at this time, the officials of the Stationery Office were not masters in their own house:

> They are exposed to the insatiable extravagance of public departments on the one hand and the short-sighted and ill-informed control of the Treasury on the other. They are annually harried for their good by the Select Committee of the House of Commons on Publications. No commercial undertaking could hope to succeed under these conditions; and the Stationery Office probably makes the best of a difficult situation.

The new Supplies Division made a move ahead of its time when in 1927 it began to alter all units of issue to a decimal base in preparation for the introduction of a mechanical accounting system. This required purchase in tens and hundreds instead of the conventional dozens and grosses, and contractors resisted having to change traditional packing methods for one customer, however large. The Stationery Office was among the first Government Departments to see and apply the advantages of mechanical (punched-card) accounting techniques to administrative work. The installation not only took over Supplies Division's stock recording and analysis work but also all the main accounting processes, the job-costing requirements of the printing works and the statistical information needed by Publications Division.

The modernization of office systems which began in 1927 was maintained the following year by the introduction of small offset-litho printing machinery. Copiers, dictation machines, addressing machines and a wide variety of adding and calculating equipment followed.

Supplies Division well knew that the very nature of Government work meant they must be prepared for the unforeseen event which necessitated an urgent purchase of paper on a big scale. The building of good relations with paper contractors ensured a quick response when the crisis came. The sending of a defence force to Shanghai in 1927, for instance, meant that a large quantity of stationery had to be ordered on a Saturday for despatch the following day. Warehouse staff were called in by telegram and the consignment of 38 tons was ready on time. Nevertheless, for more than a decade after the end of the Great War, at a time when prices steadily fell, Supplies Division adopted a policy of careful buying to make sure that overstocking did not lead to financial loss.

At the end of 1929 the Stationery Office was represented at the Conference of the Association of Special Libraries at Cambridge, at which careful consideration was given to the proposed Berne scheme to limit paper stocked to two or three large sizes. At the time the Stationery Office felt this would be too restricting for books and forms since ratio of width to depth would remain the same even when the sheets were divided, and would prevent economical use of printing machines. Later, however, in the 1950s, the Stationery Office pioneered the introduction of standard paper sizes for Government work.

The Stationery Office had an interest in libraries other than paper, namely binding. In 1923 the Controller had been asked by Sir Frederick Kenyon, Director of the British Museum in London which housed its famous Library, to help prepare a new contract under which Eyre & Spottiswoode would continue to operate the Library's Bindery on British Museum premises. Four years later in August 1927 the Stationery Office took over the Bindery. They were obliged to retain the staff and existing rates of pay, but they made many changes in production methods and introduced machinery to replace much of the handwork. This helped to reduce costs, but an even greater saving was made in 1929 with the introduction of two oversewing machines. The larger machine for newspapers was the only one at that time in this country, and had been declared an impossibility until one was seen working in the Congressional Library in Washington.

Newspapers which formerly took a girl four and a half hours to bind were now being sewn on the machine in 15 minutes.

Apprentices were introduced who learnt the special requirements of the British Museum and continued a traditional craft which had remained unchanged for many years, undertaking the restoration and conservation of priceless documents and manuscripts. In 1932 newspaper work was transferred to the new British Museum building at Colindale, where a National Newspaper Library was established.

### Aiming to reduce turnover

Attempts by the Stationery Office to operate more economically never suited *every* customer. As William Codling's deputy Norman Scorgie remarked, 'there is something about stationery, printing and publicity work generally which seems to attract much more than its fair share of public attention in relation to the actual cost of it in the nation's bill'. It was fallacious, he told the Committee on National Expenditure in 1931, in the midst of the Economic Crisis, to compare the Stationery Office with a supply organization such as a large retail store on the basis of the ratio of staff to turnover. Both were concerned to buy economically and supply the most efficient articles, but the store aimed at a big turnover, and the bigger it was the lower the percentage of overhead charges. 'The aim of the Stationery Office is in brief to reduce turnover, and the better and more efficient the scrutiny of demands, the higher the percentage of overhead charges to turnover is likely to be.'

And there was always that emergency which could never be costed in strictly commercial terms. At half past nine in the evening on 30 June 1932 William Codling received a telephone call to say the Chancellor of the Exchequer had just announced the War Loan Conversion scheme, for the printing of whose application forms he had been preparing in secret for many weeks. Codling immediately phoned the Harrow Press, and by five o'clock the following day 16 million forms of 12 kinds in

varying quantities had been printed and despatched to the
Savings Bank Department at South Kensington, to the Money
Order Department at Holloway, and to the Bank of England,
where an army of clerks were waiting to collate the forms and put
them into three million previously addressed envelopes. The
whole job took 24 hours and 74 tons of paper. Every stockholder
received an application form through the post not later than the
morning of Saturday, 2 July.

To achieve greater awareness of what a call on Stationery
Office services of this sort meant, and how it was met, a proposal
was made that customer relations would be improved by holding
an annual conference of Clerks of Stationery who ordered their
Department's requirements from Supplies Division. The first of
these conferences, held in 1933, aroused so much interest that 65
departmental representatives attended, which was very gratifying
to William Codling who chaired it.

More spectacular than the routine supply operation geared to
keep the wheels of Government moving smoothly, was publication, which had grown to between 4,000 and 6,000 titles a year in
the mid-1930s, including booklets promoting research, and
monographs on medical, industrial, technical, meteorological
and scientific subjects. Studies on social problems, the drink
trade, the treatment of crime, lotteries and betting, broadcasting
and television, parks and forests sold strongly as source material
for students, and books on physical training and preserving fruit
were snapped up as practical manuals. The first issue of *The
Highway Code* in 1931 had been a major operation, and in July
1935 Northern Area Branch at Manchester were given the job of
issuing two-and-three-quarter million copies of the revised
edition to postmasters and postmistresses throughout England
and Wales.

In contrast to the non-stop production of this best-seller was
the one-off operation which the Stationery Office mounted for the
coronation of His Majesty King George VI in 1937. Among the
70 items His Majesty's Stationery Office had to produce were the
Earl Marshal's 5,500 letters enclosing an invitation, dress
instructions for clergy, mayors and pages, orders about robes,
1,218 chair cards, 1,200 rehearsal tickets and 5,100 'Slips re

Time 6 am'. Each item, however trivial, was immaculately designed.

The coronation came at a time when the Stationery Office was giving much greater attention to typographical design. The fresh approach was certainly responsible for attracting new readers to publications whose bland form of presentation had for so long been a stock-in-trade of music hall comedians and jokesters on 'the wireless'. 'So it has come about' stated a *Times* leader in May 1937 'that the Blue Book, once the Cinderella of literature, is being transformed into the fairy princess whose court never lacks attentive suitors.' Changes in style were illustrated in the New and Old exhibition at the opening of the refurbished Kingsway Sale Office in 1938. Receipts from bookshop sales rose from £150,000 a year in the early 1920s to nearly double that figure in 1939.

The effects of modernization were perhaps rather less notice-able behind the scenes: James Turner (later an Assistant Controller), who came to Princes Street (Storey's Gate) as a Printing Clerk at £250 a year in 1938, recollected:

> Along one half of the front of the building ran the Controller's quarters from which, as one passed by, sometimes emerged the smell of breakfast cooking. These quarters were a 'holy of holies', never at any time entered by the common herd. The Controller made his pronouncements through the Establishment Officer (an aloof and dignified personage), and downwards through Heads of Divisions, etc. Long corridors ran along the inside walls of the building and at intervals there were desks holding attendance books, ink pot and pen. Blue ink started the day and soon after the official starting time (10 am when I commenced duty) the ink was changed to red in order to identify late-comers. After signing, everyone made sure that the pen was well charged with blue ink in order to assist anyone who arrived just after the colour change. Habitual late-comers spat on the pen nib in the hope of at least achieving a watery-blue signature. To use a fountain pen (Biro not yet invented!) warranted drastic punishment.

Office hours were now ten to five rather than ten to four. It was not considered 'form' to arrive in Princes Street either early or late, and staff assembled just before Big Ben started to chime, and were all inside signing in by the time the tenth stroke had reverberated across Parliament Square. The frock coats had given way to lounge suits 'of sober hue', though on Saturday morning it was permissible to wear a sports jacket and even a collar-attached shirt, but any man who turned up without a tie was left in no doubt that he had gone too far!

By the mid 1930s the 150-year-old Stationery Office employed over 3,000 staff; more than 2,000 were 'industrial' staff who were paid by the hour and had shorter holidays and fewer privileges than most of the 'office' staff. Two-thirds of these industrials worked in the two big printing works at Harrow and Southwark, and in the small Presses. Almost all the others were in the warehouses: these large depots handled the receipt and storage of the bulk deliveries of paper and office requisites, and the issuing of supplies to customers. Some worked in the forms stores, where bulk supplies of forms used by individual Departments were kept. These forms were issued on demand to individual offices operated by those Departments throughout the United Kingdom, thereby relieving them of a substantial housekeeping job.

Both the Supplies Division and the Printing and Binding Division were able to achieve considerable economies by spotting the possibilities for standardization: for example, in the 1920s Departments were using no less than 89 different types of book to record staff attendance, but by 1936 only one standard book was issued.

Areas which expanded considerably during this period were the Duplicating Branch and the Laboratory in Shepherdess Walk and Cornwall House respectively. Demand on Duplicating services increased so much that the Branch became a freestanding Division which eventually outgrew the Shepherdess Walk building.

Meanwhile the publishing business of between four and six thousand titles a year produced annual sales through Government sale offices running at over £200,000. But the business did not justify opening more shops for direct selling than the existing five in London, Manchester, Edinburgh, Belfast and Cardiff. Sales to the book trade continued to develop and, along with most of the mail-order requirements of business and private customers, these were carried out from Cornwall House in London.

## *Identity cards by destroyer*

The secret printing of 78 million ration books of food, clothing and petrol coupons at Harrow Press as a precautionary measure (begun in December 1938 and completed in August 1939) was a pointer to the events which soon halted the growth of Government publishing. Attention was switched to producing handbooks on Air Raid Precautions, which sold in their millions, and other topical publications designed to help the civilian population live through a war which affected them as no other had ever done.

At the end of 1938 Supplies Division formulated their own emergency measures and contingency plans. Should evacuation from London prove necessary, the centre for the Supplies Division operation would be moved to Manchester and to the new Regional Office, Western Area Branch, which had been set up to provide an additional store for printing paper in case the London warehouse was knocked out by enemy action. A disused multi-storey chocolate factory in Bristol was taken over for the purpose and provided space for the relocation of other activities when necessary. Staff on holiday at the end of August 1939 were recalled by telegram and ordered to hold themselves in readiness at home until the end of their holiday period. They were sent a postal draft for £5 to get themselves to Bristol or Manchester. In the event, Supplies Division remained in London, and the postal drafts were cancelled before their encashment date.

Throughout the six years of war – and indeed for another eight years after it ended – procurement of most items was extremely difficult. Some raw materials such as paper and steel could be obtained only under licence in very limited quantity; others such as rubber could not be obtained at all. Every item was rationed and some were taken off stock altogether. However the needs of all essential services, particularly the supply of paper for printing and binding, were met. As the demand for print went up, the capacity to produce it went down. The Luftwaffe destroyed the Pocock Street Press in December 1940, and the printing of *Hansard* and Parliamentary Papers was shifted to new premises in Drury Lane.

Non-Parliamentary publishing was virtually suspended on the outbreak of war in September 1939, until the Minister of Information asked the Stationery Office to produce a series of morale-raising publications on wartime exploits. The first of these, Hilary Saunders' *The Battle of Britain* (3*d* plain, 6*d* illustrated) sold more than four million in the UK and another two million in America and elsewhere. *Bomber Command, Battle of Egypt* and *Front Line 1940–41* were just three of nine titles that sold more than one million copies. And that in spite of the Stationery Office abiding strictly (some said more than strictly) to the economy standards of production devised by commercial publishers to economize in paper consumption. An Economy Section was created in Printing and Binding Division to solve the problems arising from the reduction of paper sizes. One day an irate officer of the Ministry of Food came to Princes Street to complain of the insufficient space left for butchers to fill in the required details in a newly designed form. When the Economy Section officer demonstrated in his neat and precise handwriting how easily the form could be completed, the man from the Food Ministry pointed out that the beefy men in straw hats and striped aprons who did the filling-in used skewers dipped in blood.

It was not the size of the paper but the amount of it made available to the Stationery Office which roused the envy of the commercial houses, who scolded it for entering the field of general publishing which was 'not one of the functions for which the Office was created'. The Controller had the better of them by the powers he was given under the Defence Regulations to give any printer directions and fix their remuneration. However the Stationery Office had considerable difficulty in obtaining all the paper and other items it needed, and was subject to licensing and other restrictions like everyone else.

A Press was set up at Manchester in 1942 as a fallback for the printing of ration books at Harrow. Northern Area Branch became responsible for delivering identity cards by lorry in bulk – a cargo which risked hijacking in view of their value on the black market. An army staff officer always travelled in the front seat. Getting them safely to Belfast presented a problem. The Royal Navy, Western Approaches, agreed to put a destroyer at the disposal of the Stationery Office to collect the identity cards from the lorry at Liverpool Docks. 'All was safely stowed under lock and key, and the destroyer was met at Belfast in the early hours. After which the destroyer went off to the Atlantic looking for submarines.' Manchester became more and more committed to the administration of contract printing as the war progressed, particularly the supply of aircraft manuals for the Ministry of Aircraft Production housed in hotels in Harrogate, to which a Stationery Office liaison officer was appointed. When Liverpool was bombed and several Government offices destroyed, Manchester rushed in 100 typewriters and replaced all the lost forms within 48 hours.

Sir William Codling and his staff stayed at Princes Street until 1942, the year when he retired after 43 years in the Stationery Office and 23 at the helm. He had been knighted in 1935 and seen the staff grow from 150 to 5,000. One of his last jobs was to supervise publication in December 1942 of the famous 120,000-word *Beveridge Report*, which outlined a unified system of social insurance and paved the way for the Welfare State.

The move from the one-time Queen Anne Mews beside Westminster Hospital was cautionary. If a bomb had landed in the courtyard of that 250-year-old building the whole fabric would have collapsed. So near to the Palace and Abbey of Westminster, it was lucky to have escaped for as long as it did. Certain staff had to be on duty there all night every night on a rota, and others had to report as fire-watchers to patrol the roof. Damage was negligible. Water and not flames gave vent when an incendiary bomb fell between a wall and a radiator one night. It failed to ignite, but yanking the radiator from its pipe caused a flood. One afternoon a medium-sized bomb fell into the fire-fighters' sandpit and showered sand over office windows. The only injuries were from staff bumping their heads as they dived under their desks.

Withdrawal from the lofty, wooden-beamed quarters of Princes Street, with those floors covered with dingy 'battleship' brown linoleum, was more than defensive. Up to the last week uniformed messengers brought senior officers their daily coal allowances and stoked their fires as their predecessors had done for the Grade One Clerks of McCulloch and Digby Pigott; and the move in 1942, from an environment where such tradition still lingered to the plush glass and chromium of the new office block known as Keysign House opposite Selfridges in Oxford Street, had a psychological effect which transcended the physical transfer, and did much to modernize the Stationery Office's outlook and action.

CHAPTER 6

# Breaking the mould

## 1943 – 1968

*From Oxford Street to Holborn Viaduct*

Maintaining the service to Government Departments, local
authorities and the general public in wartime needed a Controller
who knew the system backwards and had the authority to make
quick decisions, knowing they would be promptly acted on. Such
a man was ex-lawyer Norman Scorgie who had taken over from
Sir William Codling at the end of 1942. He had served the
Stationery Office for nearly a quarter of a century as Deputy
Controller. When he gave the staff an occasional address, one
member thought him reminiscent of Lord Birkenhead:

> The quiet opening, the measured development of a theme and finally the
> crescendo of polished wit, all of which with nonchalant puffs at his cigar.
> On one occasion he concluded by saying that there were two posts in the
> office which were purely ornamental, the one that of Controller, the other
> that of the doorkeeper.

He poked fun at jargon, but to make sure it did not lead to
misunderstanding he circulated memorandums with explana-
tions few would forget. Buying a bag of apples which turned out
to be pears, for instance, was 'nugatory expenditure'; if they were
apples but rotten, that was 'constructive loss'.

The new Controller was soon having to apply his mind not
only to the requirements of the wartime home front but the future
needs of a crippled Germany, where in 1944 the Thousand Year
Reich looked like collapsing at the end of its first decade. In that
year arrangements for the control of the country after its
surrender were well advanced, and Norman Scorgie had

recommended setting up a mini-Stationery Office to advise the British element of the German Control Commission. By February 1945 however wires had got hopelessly crossed. A Mr Parkes had been told to organize a Pulp, Paper, Printing and Allied Trades Division within a Textile and Light Industries Branch of the Commission and a Mr Grant at the Post Office had been asked to run the State printing industry, because in Germany it came under the Reich Minister for Posts. Scorgie said that the Stationery Office had no staff to help in German state printing works; he could do no more than supply an adviser to Control HQ as he had suggested in November 1944. 'Still less' he told them 'am I enamoured of the idea of helping Parkes to run it as a textile industry in competition with Grant who wants to run it as a postal service.' He advised Parkes to get in touch with the British Federation of Master Printers, which he did.

In 1944 Vacher & Sons, the old printing firm at The Sign of the Red Pale in Great Smith Street, Westminster, on the site where Caxton had his printing press, ran into financial problems. For a few years the works were leased by the Stationery Office as a back-up for Parliamentary printing. In 1944 too the Stationery Office took over from J.B. Nichols & Sons the Press they had run in Abbey Orchard Street, Westminster, since 1897. Nichols had been founded however by one William Bowyer as long ago as 1699, and in 1729 the Speaker appointed Bowyer printer of the *Votes and Proceedings* of the House of Commons. The firm, later as Bowyer & Nichols and from 1801 as John Nichols & Son, held the contract for 200 years. Under the Stationery Office the Abbey Orchard Street Press continued to print *Votes and Proceedings*.

Pressures on the Stationery Office in the immediate post-war years came from many directions. An example of the unexpected came from *Hansard*, the verbatim record of Parliamentary debates which had to be printed overnight so as to be on the breakfast tables of Members of Parliament in London the next day. The well-known broadcaster Commander (later Sir) Stephen King-Hall had long urged wider circulation in the interests of public information, seeking a price reduction to threepence a copy in 1943 with the hope of quadrupling the then sales of 2,500 copies. Neither objective was achieved, and in 1944

King-Hall set up the 'Friends of Hansard', later to become the 'Hansard Society'. The combination of their efforts, the shortage of newsprint and space for press reporting, and the public hunger for details of Government proposals for post-war changes, had an astonishing effect. By 1946 sales of the Commons *Hansard* topped 22,000 daily and the Stationery Office never failed to produce the larger quantity on time. Then newspapers got bigger and their reporting of the debates more comprehensive. By 1947 the circulation of *Hansard* was down to 19,000 and went on dropping steadily. By 1956 it had fallen to 5,000.

The sales organization was expanded. New sale offices were opened in Bristol (1947) and Birmingham (1948), and in 1949 a second shop in central London at Keysign House (later closed on economic grounds). Drab styles of fitment and display gave way to commercial standards. Mail order business grew, and standing order and subscription services rapidly expanded. The principle of direct official selling was established beyond question. But a third of the business went through wholesale and retail trade outlets. More than 2,000 booksellers did regular business with the Stationery Office, and this network was of great value when published material of wide public interest needed to be made available quickly throughout the country. Trade discount margins were treated more flexibly in keeping with changing practices in the book trade. Representatives of the Stationery Office began attending the Annual Conference of the Booksellers' Association.

The war had given great impetus to duplicating and photocopying and a Co-ordinator of Reproduction (later Reprographic) Services was appointed in 1950 to evaluate the large variety of reprographic equipment now being manufactured, and to advise Government Departments and the purchasing sections of Supplies Division which of them would best suit a customer's requirements.

Before retiring in 1949 Sir Norman Scorgie, who had been a signatory of the 1922 Report of the Committee on Type Faces and Display for Governmental Printing, oversaw the development of a better staffed and equipped Layout and Design Section under the guidance of Francis Meynell, the distinguished British book designer, whom he brought in as Honorary Typographical Adviser.

Meynell chose Harry Carter, who had been production manager of his Nonesuch Press, to manage 'L', as it was known, and the revitalized unit began operating in February 1946. It was answerable to William Cox, Director of Publications. A different typeface, 'Times Roman', was introduced for Parliamentary printing, the change being delayed for *Hansard*, not at the request of the Leader of the Commons but of Foreign Secretary Ernest Bevin, who much preferred the existing 'Old Style'.

The new Controller, Sir Gordon Welch, who served from 1949 to 1953, had to handle the problems created by the continuation of the Ministry of Information into peacetime as the Central Office of Information (COI). To avoid confusion, the respective roles of the two agencies had been defined in 1946. The COI was to be responsible for the editing and design of Departments' requirements for 'publicity material': 'On questions of presentation the COI can be regarded as the expert.' Overlap remained however.

The commercial lithographic Press of Malby and Sons in central London which had been acquired in 1946 moved to Alperton in West London in 1951. It was then known as Manor Farm Press, combining two units, one for lithography and the other for photogravure. In the latter part of the war petrol coupons and National Savings certificates had been printed letterpress by contractor, and so easily forged. It was therefore decided that security documents such as National Insurance stamps, road vehicle licences, etc., should be produced at Manor Farm Press by photogravure because this process was difficult to forge and was used only by a very few private sector firms. With the later switch from National Insurance stamps to collection of National Insurance through the Inland Revenue, the major part of the photogravure work was removed.

The demands of the expanded Scottish Departments led to the opening in 1950 of a new Stationery Office warehouse of 75,000 square feet at Sighthill Industrial Estate on the outskirts of Edinburgh. It was the first pre-stressed concrete multi-storey building to be built in Europe. The following year the Stationery

Office established a bindery to cater for the binding requirements of the National Library of Scotland. In 1951 too the head office at Keysign House, Oxford Street, to which the Controller and his staff had moved from Princes Street in 1942, was itself vacated, and headquarters established at the newly built Atlantic House on Holborn Viaduct.

## Coronation and competence

Preparations for the coronation of Queen Elizabeth in 1953 involved a great deal of work, not only for the graphic designers of what was once more *Her* Majesty's Stationery Office but for most parts of the Office. Planning began in earnest in May 1952, beginning with a study of the precedents of previous coronations. On those occasions most of the layout work had been done by the printers: now the Stationery Office Layout Section was able to play a significant role, especially on the 80 different jobs ordered by the Earl Marshal. Much of the work was intricate, such as the series of admission cards in 72 kinds coded by colour and design to show the status of guests and their places. The main invitation called for special attention: designs were solicited not only from artists associated with the College of Arms, but also from distinguished independent artists and the Stationery Office itself. The final choice by Garter King of Arms was a combination of a decorative border by Miss Joan Hassall and wording drawn by the Stationery Office artist Mr S.B. Stead.

To enhance the publicity and sales promotion role of Publications Division (a 'publisher' with no editorial responsibility or power to select authors or subjects) a Publicity Committee was set up in 1950 with co-opted expertise from COI. The Stationery Office had no complete monopoly for the sale of official publications. Certain of its specialist customers, such as the Patent Office, sold their own publications directly to the public. The Sir Ernest Gowers's classic *Plain Words*, which was first published by the Stationery Office in 1948, went on to secure worldwide sales of more than one and a quarter million copies, and was also published in both Penguin and Book Club editions.

From 1950 onwards the Publishers Association and individual publishers were more than ever suspicious of what they regarded as an undesirable extension of Government publishing – the 1954 edition of *The ABC of Cookery* and *The History of Light Cars* of 1958 being particular subjects of complaint. Moreover the Stationery Office began to sell in its general bookshops attractive Christmas cards formerly only sold by museums and galleries. In the eyes of the trade this was unfair competition at low and subsidized prices: Stationery Office publications did not have to meet official authorship costs and royalties, or show a profit, though the aim of course was not to make a loss overall. The Stationery Office encouraged official publishing which would sell; and a considerable amount of suitable material was to be found in museums and art galleries. Nothing better illustrated the confidence which it had in its publishing position and competence than the major series of War Histories which it began to publish in the 1950s. There were doubts both in Departments and at high levels in Whitehall about the Stationery Office's ability to take on such a professional publishing job and to distribute, particularly overseas, and pressures were exercised to co-publish with a well-known commercial publisher. Such arrangements were made for one series, but the Stationery Office was able to demonstrate that it could do at least as well as, if not better than, its commercial partner.

No publisher objected to the Stationery Office publishing *The Highway Code*, still selling four million copies at a penny in 1956, in the knowledge that they were not lumbered willy-nilly with having to market *Horse Flies of the Ethiopian Region*, *Seats for Female Shop Assistants*, or *The Measurement of Small Holes* (translated from the Russian). And though the 1,300,000 copies sold of *The Rent Act And You* (1957) at sixpence, and the 410,000 copies of *The Pound and Our Future* (1957) also at sixpence, were enviable sales, few would have questioned their place in a Stationery Office list. Despite the emphasis on the popular 'glossy' end of the Stationery Office's publishing activity, with colourful titles from the Victoria & Albert Museum, the Ministry of Works and the Science Museum, many dramatic sales successes came from more cheaply produced Parliamentary publications such as the eagerly awaited Denning Report on the Profumo Affair.

The Stationery Office also acted as UK sales agent for the publications of many international bodies including the United Nations, UNESCO, the World Health Organization and the OECD, while its own bookshops were allowed to stock and sell those of organizations such as the National Trust and the British Travel Association which were of particular local interest.

There was a considerable overseas market for British Government publications. By 1956 the Stationery Office had 34 official selling agents in 25 countries and a stand at the international Frankfurt Book Fair. The bookselling agency operated by British Information Services in New York was augmented in 1961 by a Stationery Office manager. Changes in Stationery Office publishing techniques and the cultivation of overseas agents developed the experience gained with the selling of the popular wartime publications.

The sale of publications (6,360 new titles in 1958) was the only activity for which the Stationery Office had to produce a 'commercial account'. It had done so since 1924, though it was not asked for one between 1939 and 1945. No such account was ever demanded for the total publishing activity of the Stationery Office because of the impracticability of stock-taking with many tens of thousands of different titles and the 'free' supply of copies for official use.

The new Controller, Sir John Simpson, who succeeded Sir Gordon Welch in 1954, believed that the Stationery Office had enough on its hands without extending its service beyond 'the system'. He said as much to the House of Commons Select Committee on Estimates, which in 1956 examined the activities of the Stationery Office. Any increased responsibilities, he said, would create difficulty. Large additional premises would be necessary to house the increased stocks and staff. He believed there was an optimum size for such an organization, and beyond that the benefits of large-scale purchase and supply were not increased. There were exceptions however; the hospital authorities in the National Health Service, and several other non-Exchequer bodies such as the Atomic Energy Authority and the

British Council whom the Stationery Office supplied on repayment under its Appropriation in Aid account.

In their report, published in 1957, the Select Committee
recommended that the services of the Stationery Office should be
more logically defined, and criticized the piecemeal extension of
services to bodies outside the strict limits of central Government.
On the other hand they suggested there was scope for extending
them in both the supply and publishing fields to existing
customers. The Office should be released from the 'one-third'
proportion which had originated from the Gretton Committee of
1927. There was difficulty in obtaining tenders and securing
timely work from the trade under contracts, and a shortage of
recruits for direct production. Incentive schemes and a possible
increase in customers' own in-house reprographic production
units were seen as alleviations.

Overall the Committee commented favourably on the competence and keenness of the Stationery Office staff. They were of
the opinion that 'the Stationery Office is performing its considerable functions with efficiency and economy'.


## Eight Presses print a third

In the 1950s the Stationery Office's basic printing and binding
was carried out at eight factories. These in-house Presses printed
about a third of the work which the Stationery Office was asked
to undertake every year. The rest was competed for by 1,700
approved commercial printers divided into 48 categories according to their capacity and the types of work for which they were
best fitted. They won their contracts by competitive tendering in
reply to individual invitations. The winner was 'the lowest
acceptable tender', not the lowest price. The Stationery Office
supplied the paper – some 30,000 tons of it every year bought
directly from manufacturers – because this had been proved to be
more economical for almost all types of work.

Harrow Press with 1,000 staff and 246,000 square feet of floor
space was the largest, using many thousands of tons of paper a
year, mostly for Secret, Confidential and Security printing –

postal orders, passports, excise duty stamps, savings certificates, radio and television licences – and long runs such as telephone directories (12 million a year) and Pay As You Earn tax tables, of which 14½ million had to be printed every time there was a tax change. For another eight years of austerity after the Allies won the war, Harrow Press went on printing 60 million ration books, all serially numbered and strictly security-controlled, requiring very competent organization and care by everyone concerned.

Secret and Confidential lithographic printing was done at Manor Farm Press where there were 140 staff. The Drury Lane Press (410 staff) did mainly Parliamentary work, as did the Abbey Orchard Street Press (90). The 260 at the Manchester Press did pension and allowance books, and from 1956 the £1 and £2 Premium Savings Bonds which presented severe technical problems. The 100 at the Foreign Office Press did Secret work, not only for the FO but for the Treasury and the Ministry of Defence; the War Office Press (65) did its own Secret work and overflow jobs from the FO; the Dunstable Press with a staff of ten did weather maps and charts for the Meteorological Office. These professionals had high standards of accuracy, and there were few embarrassing errors of the kind that occurred in the *London Gazette* in 1930, when a notice on the voluntary winding up of The British Macaroni Co Ltd appeared under the heading 'The British Marconi Co Ltd'. Marconi were not amused.

The Meteorological Office Press, which had been transferred from Cornwall House to Dunstable in 1941, was moved again in 1961 to Bracknell, the new headquarters of the Meteorological Office, and continued its work for 20 years (closing in 1981). The India Office Press had been closed down in October 1938, but the War Office Press in the basement of the Whitehall building, which the Stationery Office had taken over from Harrisons in 1922 and operated throughout the war, was not closed down until 1961 when its Confidential work was transferred to the new St Stephen's Parliamentary Press.

The eight Stationery Office Presses and five binderies were fully stretched. In addition branch offices to provide local duplicating and addressing facilities for Departments in the provinces were opened in Leeds and Nottingham in 1948, in

Newcastle in 1949, in Reading and Cambridge in 1950, and in Birmingham in 1951.

The opening of St Stephen's Parliamentary Press by the Speaker of the House of Commons on 23 October 1961 marked the bringing together under one roof for the first time of all the Stationery Office's Parliamentary printing. All the work done at the Abbey Orchard Street and Drury Lane Presses was transferred to it. The new Press occupied a total floor space of 114,000 square feet. Built on the site of the former Stationery Office warehouse next door to the old Parliamentary Press in Pocock Street, which had been destroyed in the war, it cost £400,000. Some 600 staff were employed at the outset, but with the growth of Parliamentary business over the next two decades this grew to 700. Commons and Lords *Hansards* were produced overnight by traditional hot-metal Linotype and Monotype typesetting techniques and hand composition; and also the *London Gazette*, Bills and Acts of Parliament, the Vote Bundle and Lords Minute, Command Papers, Order Papers, White Papers and Ministerial Orders. Some of these came at predictable intervals, others were often needed unpredictably urgently. The fluctuating demand not unnaturally created problems of production control and working conditions, both during the night and during the Recess.

Production of *Hansard* was undertaken as a service to Parliament with no hope of recovering the full cost, though exceptional items such as the 2,875 copies sold at a shilling a time carrying the Lords' debate on *Lady Chatterley's Lover* should have helped. The long series of Command Papers on policy issues were also a reliable source of income. Moreover each White Paper was consistent in style and a worthy example of good printing. In 1954 Layout Section was encouraged to introduce a variety of type-faces and brightly coloured covers to enhance non-Parliamentary publications such as the series of booklets for the Victoria & Albert Museum, Ministry of Works *Guides* to ancient monuments, and the Science Museum's *History of Sailing Ships*. The Stationery Office always held that Government Departments should have their own typographical 'tones of voice'. In 1959 six Stationery Office publications were selected for awards at the Book Design Exhibition sponsored by the National Book League, and similar successes were frequently achieved in following years (including five in 1985).

In 1959 too an inter-Departmental Committee recommended that Government Departments should be allowed to do their own reprographic work. This signalled the eventual decline of Stationery Office reprographic services but on the other hand paved the way for the Office to supply greatly increased quantities of reprographic equipment to Departments.

In 1960 the Stationery Office pioneered the first of a series of periodic meetings between Government printers from all over the world. It was held in the British consulate at Dusseldorf at the time of the International Printing Fair, and was attended by Stationery Office counterparts in the USA, Canada, Australia, West Germany, France, Holland and many other countries. Subsequent meetings have been held every three or four years. A Government Printers' Newsletter was instituted by the Stationery Office in 1980.

In the early 1960s six noiseless typewriters were ordered as part of the supplies kept in readiness for the state funeral of Sir Winston Churchill who on 30 November 1964 celebrated his 90th birthday. When, two months later, the day of national mourning took place, 'Exercise Hopenot', as it was called, had been carried out as planned and the invitations to the funeral typed on those silent keyboards.

## On the move

In the mid 1950s the Stationery Office had been asked to participate in the move of Government work out of London, and it agreed to replace the big duplicating and addressing unit in Shepherdess Walk with a new custom-built centre in the New Town at Basildon, opened in 1964.

This might have been thought to be sufficient re-location for the Stationery Office, but at the end of 1962 came a much more rigorous examination of the need for Civil Service units to remain in London. In 1963 Sir Percy Faulkner, who had by then succeeded Sir John Simpson as Controller, discussed possibilities for the dispersal of Stationery Office activities from London with Sir Gilbert Flemming, who had been appointed as overlord of the Government drive to transfer jobs to the provinces. They agreed that virtually all the headquarters functions of the Stationery Office, except for the Publications and Printing Works Divisions, could be moved without unacceptable loss of efficiency. But to carry out so big an upheaval without distress and inefficiency needed wider consultation, and the views of the staff were canvassed. If head office had to move out of London, where should it move to? Eleven possible locations were considered and visits made to nine of them; eventually the list was whittled down to three – Basingstoke, Norwich and Swindon. Management said it would move to whichever of these locations was the preference of a majority of the staff and the vote went decisively in favour of Norwich. This choice was announced in September 1964, when Sir Percy Faulkner wrote: 'This move is one of the most important events in the life of the Stationery Office'. The first few volunteers began working there in June 1966; the first large move was in May 1967 but the main migration, under the watchful eye of the new Controller, Harry Pitchforth, took place between June and November 1968. Stationery Office staff spread over the whole of Britain now numbered 7,500, half of whom were 'industrials'. It was around this time that the publishing and bookselling side of the Stationery Office adopted the acronym 'HMSO' and this soon became recognized usage for the old forms 'HM Stationery Office', or just 'the Stationery Office'.

### Into the computer age

Dispersal to Norwich held up progress in plans for further computerization, which had begun in 1958 with the installation in Atlantic House, London, of one of the first computers in Government to undertake administrative functions. The remainder of the information needed by management was mainly provided by roomfuls of punched-card machines. As a result of a Treasury Organization and Methods Report, a team was set up within the Stationery Office in 1963 to look at the possible computerization of these mechanical processes, and it was implementation of their final report, published in 1965, which was delayed by the move to Norwich. There was also the matter of the Combined Tabulating Installation (CTI), a specialized unit which had been set up in 1951. At that time the Stationery Office had been invited to take over, merge and run six punched-card installations operated domestically by other Departments; and by 1953 savings of eight staff, 12 machines and 1,000 square feet of office space had been achieved.

The late 1950s saw the beginning of an explosion in the office machinery field due in the main to the introduction of electronics, the widespread use of magnetic recording materials and the advent of electrostatic copying introduced into Britain by Rank Xerox, from whom the Stationery Office purchased its first xerography unit in 1957.

In that year there were around 120,000 machines in use in the Civil Service including typewriters, accounting machines, tabulating equipment, addressing equipment, dictating machines and computers. By the end of the 1960s this had more than doubled to over 265,000. In the same period expenditure on the purchase of machinery rose from under £1 million (£900,000) to £13.4 million, and on hire from £700,000 to £5.2 million. This growth was matched by an expansion of the maintenance service. In the 50 years since the appointment of the first mechanic in 1910 the strength of the Office Machinery Repair Service had grown to more than 100, with a qualified engineer as manager. By the end of 1966 this had doubled to 200 spread over the whole of Britain. Altogether some 200 different makes and models of machines had to be attended to. 'As the number and complexity of machines grows,' stated a memorandum of that time, 'so must the repair service keep pace; and it is a measure of the success of OMRS that, despite machine growth, repair costs are so far being contained.'

For computers in the Civil Service, the Stationery Office was the purchasing agency from the start, together with the associated software and all consumables and peripherals. In 1965 it also became responsible for buying scientific computers but soon the growth in computer purchases prompted the Government to set up the Central Computer Agency, who in 1972 took over the purchase of all but the smallest computers from HMSO.

The growing use of computers in Government Departments led to HMSO becoming involved in providing the continuous stationery and business forms associated with them. A specialist procurement unit within the newly titled Print Procurement Division was formed to provide expert advice to Government computer users on this new area of printing, and to develop procurement procedures. With the demise of Contracts Division, which had been set up in 1948, Print Procurement assumed responsibility in 1967, along with other purchasing divisions, for the preparation and award of contracts.

Print Procurement Division immediately embarked on a new and innovative trial purchasing scheme known as the Marks & Spencer Experiment. Modelled on the purchasing methods of the famous retail chain, the scheme was applied in 1968 to a range of loose-leaf and plastic binding items where there was limited competition. On proving a success it was developed into the Special Purchasing Arrangement which has become a permanent part of print procurement methods. The majority of the staff of Print Procurement Division moved from London to Norwich that July, and East Anglian printers quickly showed an increased interest in HMSO.

### Typesetting changes

The increasing size of telephone directories called for additional printing capacity – a new Press. Its location became a matter of considerable political interest. The decision reached in 1968 was that the new printing works should be at Gateshead on Tyneside and produce telephone directories by computer-assisted photo-composition. The Stationery Office had written the first of many successful typesetting programs for a computer to assist in the composition of type in 1964. The Gateshead project was a pioneering effort, in conjunction with the Post Office, to apply the theory of computer-assisted typesetting which was then very much in its infancy. At the beginning of the 1960s the Stationery Office had foreseen that the increased number of directory entries could not be handled by hot-metal printing techniques. It was a matter of planning an entirely new printing works; and if the presses were to start rolling in time, the conversion of a factory on Tyneside had to be undertaken at top speed.

Contributing to the success at Gateshead was the work which had already been done in this field by the HMSO Press in Edinburgh. It was acquired by the Stationery Office in April 1963 at a time when bookwork facilities for Government printing in Scotland were difficult to locate. The premises and plant were purchased from an old-established book printing house, J. & J. Gray, whose industrial staff, numbering then about 50, were re-engaged. Initially all printing was done by letterpress, producing mainly books, booklets and pamphlets and including high quality four-colour half-tone work. Most of it was for items originating in England and for delivery south of the Border; and the need to change telephone directories to all-figure numbering instead of named exchanges and numbers caused the Stationery Office to form a computer typesetting unit at the Edinburgh Press in 1965. As the second stage of the Edinburgh Press telephone directory project, Elliott Automation provided an on-line system to the Stationery Office's specification – a remarkable development for its time.

To concentrate on these difficult and important developments, the Stationery Office in 1966 formed a Technical Development Division, later renamed 'Technical Services Division'. A Technical Advisory Panel has operated since 1971 to monitor printing and reprographic projects in HMSO and to consider the appropriate use of new technology. Its membership is drawn from leaders in industry and research establishments. There is also close liaison with the Printing Industries Research Association: the Controller is a PIRA Council Member and HMSO nominates staff to committee and project panels.

Though the small general purpose computer system at Edinburgh Press had made a start in the comparatively new technique of computer composition, manual page make-up was still necessary. In 1969, however, a Linotron 505, which had been tested at Atlantic House, was moved to the Gateshead Press which opened in May that year, and this allowed the Post Office to supply telephone directory entries on magnetic tape instead of the conventional printer's copy. The tape was processed on a computer to add typographic information. A further tape was then produced which operated a photocomposing machine capable of composing a made-up page in two and a half minutes on film or bromide paper, which compared with the four hours needed to make up a page in hot metal. The 'Yellow Pages' Business Directories were produced, partly by photosetting from a magnetic tape, and partly from conventional copy.

To meet the requirements of the programme of computerization of pension and allowance books introduced by the Department of Health and Social Security, Manchester Press set up a Continuous Stationery Department. The complicated printing of the foils and covers of pension books, which was first done mechanically by purpose-built rotary presses, passed to the fast-running continuous stationery machines which turned out precision-printed packs for feeding into computers. These overprinted the up-to-the-minute details required to ensure correct payment to each recipient.

The Premium Bond Scheme, as well as the Post Office Giro Scheme, brought further developments, and special machinery was installed to produce Girocheques in a variety of designs in sheet, continuous or single form and with a range of numbering systems. In 1969 the introduction of a new type of British passport led to the installation of yet another purpose-built machine. In addition to Security work, Manchester Press undertook a considerable amount of miscellaneous Government printing on equipment suited to the mass production of long-run jobwork.

Computerization could not be applied to printing petrol coupons when the Government gave urgent instructions in June 1967, at the time of the Middle East War, to increase the existing stock of 10 million left over from the Suez crisis to 14 million. That was beyond the capacity of the HMSO Presses, and with no time to put the work out to tender, the order was placed with De La Rue. In fact the coupons were never used. It was what

Government was always having to do, play safe; but it often played havoc with the endeavours of service agencies such as HMSO to see there was no interruption to normal services.

There always had to be quick reaction to new demands and, just as important, no implied resentment when what was expected to be permanent proved temporary. Machines were designed and ordered for Manor Farm Press to print the road fund licence discs which were to be issued with the aid of computers from the new Vehicle Licensing Centre at Swansea. The first press was delivered, but soon the scheme was abandoned, and the plans made for floor space, staff and equipment cancelled. The arrangements were then unscrambled ready for re-deployment in the next project to come from who knows where. It was in the very nature of HMSO's brief.

With the varying demands of so many customers, resilience and resource were the key, but knowing the answers had always been the stock-in-trade of the Stationery Office. From a better-informed Civil Service, with more technically minded Clerks of Stationery, the questions tended to be more pointed; the witty comment from the touchline however was much as it had always been. As anyone who has read so far will recognize, the author of *Parkinson's Law*, in referring to Stationery Office publications, was taking his place in a long line of critics when in *The Law and the Profits* he wrote of the continents being de-forested, pulping machines worn out and paper-makers kept working day and night 'to keep up with this appalling output of literature'.

He may have been appalled by the 25 million copies of each of three 16-page books arguing the merits of, and objections to, Britain's continuing membership of the European Economic Community prior to the 1975 referendum. For HMSO staff however the speed with which this 'hot job' was carried out – possibly the fastest in relation to size ever handled – was a matter of pride. HMSO had a week to typeset and proof them under Confidential conditions, and another three to print and gather them. Contracts with some 60 printers had to be arranged in a matter of days, and the whole exercise safe-guarded against premature leaking.

CHAPTER 7

# Trials and tribulations
## 1969 – 1980

*Fulton Report recommends accountable management*

By the end of 1968 two-thirds of the HMSO headquarters staff
had moved to Norwich, and at the time this was seen as a milestone in the Department's history. But the report of the Royal
Commission on the Civil Service chaired by Lord Fulton, published in that same year, was to have even greater effect. One of
its 158 recommendations was that managers in the Civil Service
should be held responsible for their performance (measured as
objectively as possible); that for the first time the Civil Service
should apply the principles of accountable management.

It had been suggested to the Royal Commission that these
could best be introduced when the occasion arose for a
Government Department to hive off an activity to, say, an
autonomous board or a public corporation. These ideas stimu-
lated a series of studies and enquiries, one of which concerned
the Supply Division of the then Ministry of Public Building and
Works, whose activities relating to office furniture and domestic
supplies suggested the possibility of a link with HMSO's supply
functions. But first HMSO carried out studies. Consultant
accountants Cooper Brothers were invited to advise on practical
alternative accounting arrangements which would assist HMSO
in planning and controlling its activities. Their principal
recommendation was for the introduction of an integrated
budgetary control system on commercial lines.

A joint study by a team drawn from HMSO and from the Civil
Service Department followed; its 1971 report recommended a

redefinition of the aims of HMSO and considered that the application of the principles of accountable management would provide an environment in which the information provided by the sort of system suggested by the consultants would be applied most effectively. The study team also thought that even greater motivation would be provided by a move to repayment by Departments which, it felt, would achieve more effective control over expenditure on HMSO services, and by allowing Departments to go elsewhere than HMSO for service if they could demonstrate that this was advantageous.

In 1972 HMSO was told of the outcome of another study, this time on the provision of computers and computer services to Departments. At the end of the 1960s these involved not only HMSO but also the Management Services Division of the Treasury and a specialist Technical Support Unit in the Department of Trade and Industry. In April 1972 these separate units were brought together into a new unit, the Central Computer Agency, and made part of the Civil Service Department which had been created on the lines of another Fulton recommendation.

## Commitment to change

Uncertainty about the future of the rest of HMSO remained until the Prime Minister made a statement about common services in the House of Commons on 5 May 1972. This included a significant passage for HMSO:

> HM Stationery Office remains a separate Department and will continue to undertake printing, publishing and marketing of Government publications and the supply to Government Departments of office machinery, stationery and other office equipment. The Controller will be responsible for developing the application of accountable management to his organization, and the introduction of systems appropriate to a trading organization.

HMSO breathed a sigh of relief, followed by many deep breaths as it moved towards the development of accountable management. December 1972 saw a springboard for this when all the senior managers together with representatives of its trade unions spent a weekend at a specially organized conference entitled 'Commitment to Change'.

The year also saw responsibility for HMSO transferred from the Chancellor of the Exchequer to the Lord Privy Seal, the Minister responsible for the Civil Service and the Civil Service Department (CSD). But HMSO did not report to the Minister through CSD. The Controller reported directly to Ministers. Where there was no CSD responsibility, the Controller was the Minister's source of advice on such matters, for instance, as service to the public, to Government Departments and Parliament, technical developments and price changes.

The relationships between HMSO and its customers were reasonably well delineated, but to what extent was it desirable that Government Departments should be obliged to depend on them? Was it in the public interest that all of them should have to order their stationery supplies and print through the Stationery Office?

The principle involved in 'tying' Departments to HMSO was one of the matters examined by the Common Services Working Group set up in 1972. In the early years of the 19th century the principle of tying was commonly applied to all Government offices, including those who were required to pay the Stationery Office for goods and services. But for many years since the end of the Second World War non-Exchequer bodies had been free to obtain their requirements other than from HMSO. 'Tying', as a mandatory principle, had come to apply by custom and practice only to those Exchequer Departments which received their supplies from HMSO without paying for them.

The Common Services Working Group of 1972 argued on the one hand that the development of accountable management in Departments required that they should have freedom of choice in satisfying their needs as to the source of supply. But they found it a more convincing argument that it was the overall efficiency of the Civil Service which counted, and that therefore a supplying agency such as HMSO must have the opportunity to operate on a scale enabling it to achieve maximum economies. It could hardly do that if its customers were free to come and go as they pleased, or to obtain for themselves the easy or the cheap service, leaving only the difficult service to the common service supplier. Members of the Working Group also argued that there must be a concentration of expertise in the goods and services affected. The maximum efficiency, they said, could be achieved only by a close working relationship between user and supplier. The normal rule, they concluded, should be that Departments must use HMSO. However, they also agreed not only that there should be a move towards repayment but also that there were some issues which should not be entirely at the discretion of either users or suppliers, and postulated the need for some central machinery which would be responsible for approving any exceptions to the generally mandatory rule.

HMSO's relationship with Parliament also came under scrutiny. The business of the House of Commons continued to grow, and so too did the task of recording it in print, which was entrusted to the Controller by the Speaker each new Session. In 1968 the number of pages in the Vote Bundle, which HMSO had been printing since 1940, was 29,300, an increase of 150 per cent over 1964. In the same period the number of pages of Bills printed at St Stephen's Parliamentary Press doubled. Between 1964 and 1975 the total number of pages for Parliamentary work printed at the Press also doubled and the volume of work increased by 66 per cent.

Refraining from enjoining them to talk less, which Sir Norman Scorgie had once done, HMSO could do little to reduce the word output of the legislators which no one, unless privileged, could suggest was appalling without risk of contempt. And as far as non-Parliamentary wordage was concerned, the Controller (since 1969 Clifford Baylis) could – indeed had a duty to – question any demand for print and stationery, and obtain Treasury guidance on any expenditure which he thought unreasonable. Throughout its existence HMSO had been torn between the requirement to provide a service and the need to do so within its Vote. Had the time come to release it from these conflicting obligations? Did the circumstances of the 1970s demand a re-think of the whole basis of HMSO's working and a re-definition of its purpose? Could it be that simply to run it efficiently and economically no longer stood up as the all-justifying criterion it had been for 186 years?

## *Towards better management information*

HMSO pressed ahead not only with its accountable management studies, but also with the complex task of developing a new accounting system, and in May 1973 Clifford Baylis was able to tell the Public Accounts Committee that he was making steady progress towards accountable management. Finance systems were being devised to provide more prompt and accurate information for management to enable them to take better decisions and more effectively control costs and measure performance. It was hoped these would come into operation in 1975.

These early expectations of rapid progress soon had to be modified. They had been based on two premises. The first was that the main new systems for management accounting (a general ledger system, publications master file system and a job cost system) could be developed in such a time scale; this proved to be roughly correct. The second was that much of the data required as input for the new systems could be derived from HMSO's existing computer systems; it became clear that this would not be possible and that the existing systems were reaching the end of maintainable lives and would have to be reprogrammed.

These systems, dealing with needs such as contract control, payment of bills, Vote accounting and related statistics, had given excellent service. They had been developed from manual clerical procedures supported by punched-card processing in the early days. The punched-card and manual systems had been transferred on to the computer and the computer systems had gradually been extended. Much good work had been done on improving them but they had reached the stage where further modification and extension was no longer feasible. This meant that the redesign and replacement of almost every existing system would have to precede the implementation of the management accounting systems. This was a huge task.

A major team effort was launched involving members of Finance Division, representatives from the divisions who were to be the major users of the new systems, newly recruited accountants, consultants and personnel from the Central Computer Agency on secondment. New standards and policies were adopted for the tasks. They covered the design, development and documentation of the new systems. The new teams worked closely with the management of the divisions and found themselves doing much more than designing computer systems. The organization structure had to be reflected in the new master files. In tandem with the accountable management programme managers re-examined their objectives and responsibility structures and sharpened them. Though the availability of actual data to monitor the plans was a long way in the future, the new file structures were used to process planning data and estimated costs. The new cost centre structures were used to estimate overheads, replacing the notional functional costing calculations which had served the Stationery Office for so many years.

New costing policies were adopted in many areas of HMSO, using existing data as a temporary measure. In Publications Division, for example, new costing conventions were adopted which included fresh approaches to the disposal of unsold and unsaleable stocks. New methods were planned to monitor the operation of the existing standard pricing scales.

As the new information plans emerged, HMSO began the first discussions with allied service customers about repayment. A series of consultations by Treasury and HMSO with major users took place in the last half of 1974. At the same time thinking got under way on the lengthy process of implementing the switch to commercial-style practice.

The accounts for the year 1978–79 framed for the first time on this new basis showed a surplus of £2.3 million after interest, equal to about 4 per cent on average net assets. Success in achieving a given financial target depended to a large extent, said the Controller's report, on the ability to forecast both the likely level of sales and the likely level of inflation, and went on:

> It might be expected that this should be relatively easy for HMSO since the majority of its supplies are to Government Departments whose

demands must be satisfied within the cash limit on the Vote for Stationery and Printing. In practice however conflict is possible between the requirement not to exceed the cash limit and the requirement to achieve a financial target in a commercial sense. During the year of report, it became clear that measures to restrain demands from Government Departments would be needed if expenditure was to be kept within the cash limit, and Departments were told that it would not be possible to action all their demands. In the event the cash limit was underspent by some £1.6 million, and a number of demands were left unsatisfied. In 1978–79 there was nevertheless a surplus on the operating accounts.

Business with customers outside central Government was not constrained by the cash limit, but some manufacturers of proprietary goods were reluctant to supply non-Government customers at Government prices. This gave little opportunity for HMSO to expand in this area, particularly as it would have to do so without additional staff.

### Improving service to Parliament

Meanwhile the load on St Stephen's Parliamentary Press at its peak had become the equivalent of typesetting the news columns of three national daily newspapers each night, and in 1976 a Commons Committee reported that, as a result, essential Parliamentary Papers were being delivered late, particularly the Vote Bundle. The House had frequently not received the service to which it had been accustomed, and rightly expected, for the conduct of its business.

In his memorandum to the Committee Harold Glover, who had been appointed Controller in 1974, said there was no room in St Stephen's Parliamentary Press for additional machinery or operatives, and if delivery was to be restored to the customary times the daily load must be only that which the present equipment could handle. He proposed, in the long term, re-housing and re-equipping the Press with new technology, which would take three years; but to relieve immediate difficulties he suggested that the House should introduce adjustments to their procedures, such as a cut-off time for amendments to Bills.

Apart from easing the technical operation, his short-term proposals would save £58,000 a year.

One idea for relieving congestion at St Stephen's Parliamentary Press was to remove the printing of *Hansard* which had once more grown in size. In 1964 *Debates* took 16,500 pages; in 1976 26,500. Removal would mean changing the page size of *Hansard* to metric A4. Michael Foot, chairman of a Commons (Services) Committee, asked why. It was one of the first jobs of Bernard Thimont, appointed Controller in 1977, to reply. Because, he said, they wanted to establish a separate, modern Press for *Hansard* using the new, faster technology. All such machines used by commercial printers produced metric size output. If they wanted publication of *Hansard* to continue in the present size so that it would still fit their shelves, he would have to have the machines tailor-made at exorbitant cost, and their manning would not follow standard practice. Adoption of A4 would mean that British machinery could be used and that the smaller number of larger pages could be more efficiently handled. The Committee took the point and recommended the House to approve the adoption of A4. But it took three debates before the change was finally agreed by the House of Commons.

### Industrial relations for the 20th century

Considerable effort was made to develop and improve staff relations at this time, particularly with industrial staff. For the first hundred years of HMSO's existence there was no such thing as formal personnel management. No need was seen for a separate division to handle industrial personnel matters, either born of philanthropy to look after workers' interests or of fear to keep them in line. But there was no evading the trade union movement in the 20th century or the collective action which it was capable of organizing. HMSO's increased in-house printing brought it into closer contact with trade unions than ever before. With printing unions' organization based on locality, and with the need to meet Parliament's requirements by printing in central

London, HMSO was forced to take account of pay rates and manning levels in the London area, particularly in Fleet Street.

Matters came to a head toward the end of the 1960s when the fearsome complexity of HMSO's pay structures, endless arguments between the different unions representing the varied skills involved in print, and constant disruptions to production, led to attempts to rationalize and codify industrial staffs' pay and conditions at its operational establishments. Major difficulties in reaching a settlement on pay rates at HMSO Presses and binderies in 1969 caused the Government to ask the National Board for Prices and Incomes to investigate. They concluded that the causes of the dispute at that time ran deep, and required a major effort to rectify. They suggested the creation of an Industrial Relations Division within HMSO and the appointment of a Senior Industrial Relations Adviser from outside. They felt that HMSO and the trade unions should seek to evolve a system of pay and conditions which catered for the particular requirements of Government printing and binding instead of being based directly on rates negotiated in the printing industry nationally.

As a result, HMSO established an Industrial Relations Unit in 1970. Its first head, with a background in the Midlands motor industry, was well versed in the complexities of industrial relations and payment systems. Around him gathered a small group consisting of HMSO staff and seasoned practitioners engaged from industry on fixed-term contracts. Initially, as one of them reflected in 1985:

> different cultural backgrounds led to some misunderstandings, and it took time for HMSO's organisation to come to terms with the new arrival; but after inevitable teething problems of this sort, the new Division soon settled down to negotiating house agreements to cover the range of activities within the printing industry. In the early stages, line managers, protective of their powers to run things in their own way on their own patch, had to be persuaded to accept the newcomers. The Industrial Relations specialists similarly had to accept the managers' ultimate accountability.

Industrial Relations Advisers were stationed at Presses and warehouses to give on-the-spot advice and assistance while maintaining close links with the Industrial Relations head-quarters in London. In spite of this, industrial disputes became a depressingly common feature of the 1970s, reflecting general dissension in the printing industry. In 1974 National Graphical Association (NGA) members were on official strike for 11 weeks at all HMSO establishments in support of a claim for increased pay and reduction in hours. A settlement was reached on pay but a review by independent consultants of a number of firms in the private sector confirmed that there was no need for any change in hours. A major dispute with the National Society of Operative Printers & Assistants (NATSOPA) at St Stephen's Parliamentary Press in 1977 over flexible working in the machine room extended to the NGA on the question of overtime. This led to staff being put 'off-pay', and culminated in an enquiry by the Advisory, Conciliation and Arbitration Service (ACAS), who published their findings in October 1978. Outside consultants were then engaged to devise a productivity scheme which recognized the unique position of the work done at St Stephen's. After being given a trial, their scheme was rejected by the staff on the grounds that it did not bring sufficient reward. HMSO began to find it difficult to recruit qualified printing staff for its Presses, and introduced a special house payment to bridge some of the gap in basic earnings. The Government's pay policy in 1978–79 permitted the introduction of self-financing incentive schemes and HMSO took advantage of this to give higher pay for increased productivity.

*Improving service to the public*

Cornwall House, which had served as the publications distribution warehouse since the 1920s, was built massively strong and was structurally rooted in the era of cheap labour. There could be little new technology there and, indeed, there was not even headroom for fork-lift trucks! Furthermore, order-processing methods were labour-intensive and manual accounting procedures were error-prone and tedious to those who operated them. Delays in servicing orders were frequently a source of frustration and complaint and the whole operation was ripe for modernization.

HMSO opted for a new building, fitted out with the latest materials-handling equipment and sophisticated computer-controlled order-picking and accounting systems. A site convenient to Parliament and HMSO's Parliamentary Presses was secured at Nine Elms. The Publications Centre was designed and built and detailed planning for the human consequences of the move took place.

Apart from dealing with ad hoc telephone and postal orders and subscriptions, the Publications Centre would operate a sophisticated standing order service, offering customers the opportunity to receive automatically every publication published in up to 3,500 different subject categories. In addition, the Centre would service Parliament, the seven HMSO bookshops, agents, and other shops in the book-trade at home and abroad.

### Change begins to bite

In December 1979 the Treasury laid down levels of staffing for Departments which seemed to them appropriate to the Government's decision to reduce the size of the Civil Service as a whole. Because there would be fewer civil servants it was expected that fewer people would be required at HMSO to serve them. Happily the aim of the new HMSO as a commercial organization was pointing it in the same direction as, for different reasons, the Government was pointing it. Staff fell from 6,763 in April 1979 to 6,276 a year later, mainly because of the abandonment of activities seen to be less cost-effective.

For HMSO, 1978–79 was a year of transition and experiment. It was still financed by the Vote, which was £107.3 million, and most customers, though not all, were still supplied free of charge. It was however the first year in which the running of HMSO was based on the use of commercial-style management information, and the first in which it produced a commercial-style annual report.

As Bernard Thimont commented in his Controller's review which introduced the 1978–79 annual report, for many years the only accounts regularly produced on the work of HMSO had been the annual appropriation account and the annual trading accounts for the Government bookshops. He had told the General Sub-Committee of the Expenditure Committee in May 1977 that it was intended to found all the operations of his Department, whether or not they were, or could be made to be, economic, on commercial-style accounts derived from new management accounting systems. This would enable much fuller and more meaningful information to be given to Parliament than had been possible before. It was an approach welcomed by both the Expenditure Committee and the Public Accounts Committee.

In 1978–79 managers could monitor for the first time in financial terms the efficiency of their areas of responsibility, in which the notional prices charged to customers for individual items fully reflected their costs. The financial target for each activity had been to break even taking one year with another, after providing additional depreciation to cover the revaluation of fixed assets to current values and after charging interest at five per cent on the replacement value of average net assets. The overriding objective was not to exceed the cash limit on the Vote for Stationery and Printing.

As a result of a review by a staff inspection team comprising members of the Civil Service Department and HMSO in April 1978, the Accounts Division and the Finance and Planning Division were merged and became responsible under the Deputy Controller for all the financial affairs of HMSO. The first annual budgets on commercial lines were monitored to ensure consistency with the Vote through which HMSO was still being financed. In the same way, longer term forward plans were made to conform with the forecasts published in the Government's annual White Papers on public expenditure. A system of capital investment appraisal was adopted using the latest techniques of project evaluation to control capital expenditure.

Keeping within the limits of the Vote became increasingly difficult as the cost of stationery and print increased. For the last year in which HMSO was financed by it (1979–80) the remedy was to increase the Vote, to keep abreast of the cost of everything it had to buy, including salaries, fuel, and electricity, while maintaining commercial accounts to measure 'surplus' or 'deficit'. Raising the Vote from £106 million to £114 million in that year highlighted the impracticality of continuing the historic basis of operation. It was not a move likely to please the Conservative Government elected to power on a promise of cutting public expenditure.

There was radical change too in the arrangements for Northern Ireland. The agreement by which the Belfast office was administered by HMSO as an agency service to the Government of Northern Ireland, which had been revised in 1948, was replaced from 1 January 1978 by a system of full repayment. The 1948 agreement provided for the apportionment of costs of running the Northern Ireland Regional Office between the two Governments, but on a somewhat arbitrary basis. Its termination did not involve any fundamental change in the relations of the Belfast office with Government of Northern Ireland (GNI) Departments or in the type or level of service provided by HMSO. It continued to provide a publishing service for the Northern Ireland Assembly and Government Departments, and to supply stationery, office machinery and printing. The bookshop sold both UK and GNI publications, and a warehousing and distribution service was provided.

There was no formal new agreement, merely an exchange of letters between HMSO and GNI's Department of Finance. The arrangement could be varied by mutual consent at any time or be terminated by two years notice by either side. There were no agreements as such with individual GNI Departments. Though the province had no legislative body after the fall of the Northern Ireland Executive in May 1974, the Belfast office continued to act as publisher for the debates of the various bodies set up at Stormont over the years including the Northern Ireland Assembly. The Northern Ireland Act of 1974 introduced the power to legislate for Northern Ireland by Orders in Council with government through the Secretary of State; and the Controller of HMSO remained the Queen's Printer of the Northern Ireland Acts.

## Back to repayment

What Bernard Thimont described as 'probably the most fundamental change which has affected HMSO in the last century and a half' took place on 1 April 1980.

Caught between the rising tide of costs in every area of its operation and the intended static nature of the Vote which kept it afloat, HMSO had latterly been forced into the invidious position of having to decide which orders from Departments to curtail in order to keep within the cash limit. Such decisions were often purely arbitrary, because HMSO had no way of knowing what effect curtailment would have on customer Departments. But when, under the provisions of the Government Trading Funds Act of 1973, the financing of HMSO by annual Parliamentary Vote was discontinued, what the Government (the taxpayer) could afford by way of stationery and print became the collective decision of the Government Departments which had to order only what *they* could afford within *their* cash-limited annual Votes. Total HMSO expenditure found its own level. It was back to John Mayor's plan which operated until 1824, though he would have deemed it crude to regard repayment as 'trading'. The purpose of the change of 1980 was to save the taxpayer money – as had been the purpose of the change from the patent-holder system of 1786. But this time the motivation had an additional dimension. For many there was something morally irresponsible about a Government Department which did not have to pay for its goods and services, not knowing – and possibly not caring – what they cost. It was 'wrong', it was said, that they were not aware of the economic value of what they were receiving free. Not paying was seen to cultivate an unbecoming insouciance; whereas paying, it was reckoned, would concentrate the mind. And that could not be other than a Good Thing.

Such thoughts were in the minds of those who, in the final months of Edward Heath's Conservative administration, framed the Government Trading Funds Bill. This allowed a minister to direct by Order that the operations of a 'Crown Service' should be financed by a Trading Fund, established for the purpose with public money, instead of by means of an annual Vote and appropriation. He could do so only if the change appeared to him 'expedient in the interests of its improved commercial operations and public accountability'. Such an order could only be made with the consent of the Treasury and following an affirmative resolution of the House of Commons. The Act laid down ground rules for the financing and management of a Trading Fund, though not of course for running the Crown Service which it was to finance. A Fund's capital was to be provided by a loan from the National Loans Fund. The Act named four Crown Services as those to which it specifically applied; the Royal Ordnance Factories, the Royal Mint, HMSO, and the Royal Dockyards. It became law in 1973 and orders were made for the first two of these within 12 months, but as HMSO was having trouble upgrading its management information systems no one at Norwich expected to move away from Vote funding until the software and hardware could be made to function as required. In the event it was not until 29 February 1980 that the draft HMSO Trading Fund Order was laid before the House of Commons. On 24 March 1980 Paul Channon, Minister of State for the Civil Service Department, moved in the chamber the required resolution that it be approved, which it was at around two o'clock the following morning.

He said the change would put financial accountability for stationery and printing where it properly belonged, with those who generated the demands rather than with the agency whose task it was to satisfy them. While stationery and printing supplied to Parliament would continue to be provided and financed by a Vote administered by HMSO, 'in due course it may be considered appropriate for this Vote to be transferred to the responsibility of this House and another place [the House of Lords]'. But no decision about that would be taken without consulting the House. With the abolition of the Vote system Departments would see what they were spending money on, how much they were spending, and decide on a proper system of priorities. In the same way the Minister thought that in principle it was just as right for the House of Commons to have to face the consequences of knowing the cost of its stationery and printing requirements.

The HMSO Trading Fund Order (Statutory Instrument 1980 No 456) allowed for some HMSO services to be wholly or partly financed by subsidies paid from annual Votes; and from the outset this applied to two such services which, although commercially uneconomic, were undertaken as a matter of Government policy – the production of *Hansard* at high cost overnight, and sold at a price well below the full cost; and the sale of HMSO publications to certain public libraries at half the published price as had been the case for more than fifty years. These subsidies were paid from a Vote entitled 'Stationery and Printing: Payments to Her Majesty's Stationery Office' which was administered and accounted for by the Controller separately from the Trading Fund. A subsidy of £4 million was forecast to be required for *Hansard* in 1980–81, and £500,000 on sales to public libraries. The decision of the Government to subsidize *Hansard* was apart from that taken by the Parliamentary authorities to continue to have the stationery and printing supplied free on a separate, annually agreed Vote.

The Minister in winding up the debate noted that:

> we have for once – it is very rare that Governments actually do it – met unanimously and in full the recommendations of a report of the Expenditure Committee.

From 1 April 1980 therefore HMSO operated as a Trading Fund. But its new computerized management accounting system was not yet fully ready, and stop-gap measures were necessary to minimize the effect of its shortcomings on HMSO's ability to assess prices and conduct day-to-day business efficiently.

What were the ends which these troublesome systems were meant to help HMSO achieve? The Treasury spelt out the financial objectives of the Trading Fund in a minute of 22 May 1980. It would be the duty of the responsible Minister (though in effect the Controller) to break even on historical cost revenue account after the payment of interest on long-term borrowing; and to produce an operating surplus equivalent to a return on average net assets of five per cent after allowing for current cost accounting adjustments but before the payment of interest on long-term borrowing. The aim, linked to the period 1 April 1980 to 31 March 1985, would be to meet whichever of the two objectives was the higher.

More important however for the future of HMSO even than the assumption of Trading Fund status, was the change to repayment and the prospect of untying. It was a shock to many in HMSO that when Government Departments started having to pay for their goods and services, they wanted more information about what they were paying for, and instead of ordering 50 copies of a publication in case they might be needed, they cut back. The onus was now on Departments to keep within their budgets, but if HMSO was to keep them as customers it had to make sure that it, and no other supplier, provided the best buy, ever mindful however of its obligation to the Treasury to break even. The implications of this new situation were to tax the brains of the new regime for the last six of the Stationery Office's first 200 years and of the new Controller who took over from Bernard Thimont on 1 January 1981.

# PART III

## 1981 — 1986

It is hardly to be expected that any organization, with the auditor's invaluable hindsight . . . performed perfectly in every respect, although the Comptroller and Auditor General's latest report on Her Majesty's Stationery Office Trading Fund comes about as close as it is possible to that.

MR JOHN MOORE
*MP, Financial Secretary to the Treasury, in Commons debate, 24 October 1985*

# CHAPTER 8

# Clear direction

*Five Year Forward Plan*

Bill Sharp, the man appointed to succeed Thimont from 1 January 1981, had already had experience of large-scale management as the Controller of Crown Suppliers, another Government Trading Fund. This stood him in good stead in that he was able to apply the management skills acquired elsewhere to his work in HMSO. He was certain from the start that he should not only operate in the traditional role of Controller (which in his view equated to the role of the chairman of a company) but also in the capacity of the chief executive of a large and complex business. He therefore re-designated the post as Controller and Chief Executive.

The new Controller thus took control as Chief Executive of a Government Department which had always been different from conventional Government Departments but was now more different than ever. Parliament had decreed that HMSO should change from a normal Vote-funded Department to a *business* – and Sharp was determined to make a success of it. This needed the co-operation of like-minded men and women, 'people', as he said, 'with the spirit of businessmen rather than the spirit of bureaucrats'. Fortunately, the head of the HMSO Printing Group, George Macaulay, gave him full backing. Together, with the support of many others in HMSO who shared their entre-preneurial views, they gradually effected the necessary changes.

It was a tall order. Fortuitously, the new Controller and Chief Executive was greatly helped by the simultaneous appointment of

Barney Hayhoe as the Minister of State responsible for HMSO. This meant there was no need to argue the case for change with a political head who had been used to one way of running HMSO and might resist a move to the less conventional way now mooted. He was able to establish a harmonious working relationship with his Minister from the start. So long as he achieved the financial and manpower objectives settled with the Minister and kept out of political trouble, he knew that he would be left to manage the Department along the broad lines of development set out in the Five Year Forward Plan and approved each year by the Minister and the Treasury. The one exception was the Treasury's concern with the pay and conditions of service of HMSO staff which, apart from industrial staff, were determined centrally, and had to be in line with Civil Service pay generally.

The new Controller was anxious that there should be no blurring of management responsibilities for HMSO arising from the fact that his Minister's office was in the Treasury. In a memorandum to the Minister he reminded him of the note which Sir Frank Cooper had submitted to the Lord Privy Seal in 1972 when he took over ministerial responsibility for HMSO from the Chancellor of the Exchequer:

> The note is just as doctrinally relevant now that ministerial responsibility has been re-assumed by the Chancellor and delegated to you. The essential message is that HMSO is just as much a free-standing Department as, say, the Management and Personnel Office, and that you have in effect got two hats. If as HMSO Accounting Officer I therefore put something to you in confidence, it would be wrong for your office to inform the Treasury. It is for HMSO to determine whether, when and how the Treasury should be consulted, depending on the circumstances of the case. In practice of course, because of the wide-ranging responsibilities of the Treasury, both informal and formal consultations are frequent, extensive and amicable. But it is just as well that the underlying constitutional position should be borne constantly in mind.

Having a Chief Executive with a clear vision of what he wanted done and how to do it had a salutary effect on the staff who, in the light of the change to Trading Fund status, felt very apprehensive of what it might bring. Many thought that with all transactions returning to a repayment basis, the financial obligation of having to break even could never be met, and that HMSO would fail. To all who hinted that the Department had no future, the Controller proclaimed a faith in the quality of his staff from senior management down through the office to the printing Presses' shop floor.

And indeed, once they got over the cultural shock of substituting commercial for Civil Service attitudes, encouraged by a Chief Executive who, with his new management team, had won the confidence of Ministers and the Treasury, staff began to find a new sense of direction. Under the Trading Fund regime they saw their new head acting like the executive chairman of a public limited company. The new Controller told the Committee of Public Accounts in the summer of 1981:

> I found that these four businesses [of HMSO] formed a more or less loose federation, and that the corporate apparatus with frequent and regular control by the top management did not exist. I think it would be generally agreed that in an extensive agency of this size it is essential for the top management to meet together at least once a week to consider any policy issues or any problem areas – in effect to exercise a close control over the progress of the business over the financial year.

Within a few weeks he had re-instituted weekly management meetings, where decisions were taken corporately with his senior staff, formerly known as Assistant Controllers but now re-designated 'Directors-General'. These three were the nucleus of the Management Group which provided the key management control. But because he did not consider three people enough to 'spark off' in a sufficiently stimulating way, he co-opted the Director of Finance and later the Director of Personnel Services, together with the Director of Supply who reported direct to him and not via a Director-General. In addition, the Controller chaired a monthly meeting of Directors of all HMSO operating businesses and members of the Management Group, and quarterly meetings to monitor achievement of specific operational objectives – a review of warehousing for instance. He presided over the formulation of the annual budget and the Five Year Forward Plan by holding annual meetings at which the budget and planning assumptions were discussed, and through an annual performance review. He fulfilled the traditional role of his predecessors by acting as the chairman of a company, for example by seeing to it that he met influential and potential customers – Parliament, Government Departments and the rest – and the printers, office equipment manufacturers and others who were suppliers to HMSO. As Head of Department he aimed to know staff well enough several levels down to judge their capability. He did not involve himself in day-to-day operations however nor in industrial relations but concentrated, as he said, 'on men, money, organization and representational aspects'.

## *To tie or untie?*

In the decade before 1980, preparation had been made for the expected change to repayment and commercial-style accounting by heavy investment in the computer-based accounting system. Without them HMSO could never have operated as a Trading Fund, and they enabled the new management, with the increasing number of professional accountants now employed at Norwich, to build a sensitive and sophisticated set of information systems and controls. The effects of the new financial discipline would have been less severe if HMSO had been allowed to keep the privilege of the monopoly which it had enjoyed at least since the reorganization of 1824. But this was not to be the case. For the logic of replacing the Vote system by repayment required that Government Departments should be allowed to choose what they bought and where they bought it – the so-called 'untying' issue. To the existing anxieties of having to adjust to the new financial discipline therefore was added the uncertainty of the future size of HMSO's market.

The question of untying had been raised in the Commons debate of 25 March 1980 which led to approval of the HMSO Trading Fund Order. Paul Channon as Minister of State said the Government had not yet taken a decision on whether to continue to tie or to untie Departments. When the time came the matter would be decided on its merits, he said, and then went on to express his own view:

> I believe that if one has a centralized Department such as the Stationery
> Office, Government Departments should use it; otherwise there is little
> point in having it. That is a matter for Government examination.

The Interdepartmental Working Group on Tying had concluded that, in the field of Government publishing, the consid-
erations were such that further detailed examination was
necessary before recommendations could be made. As regards
the remainder of HMSO business, they did not find it possible to
draw up a precise financial balance sheet of the costs and benefits
of tying or untying. What they did find themselves able to
recommend was that Ministers should be invited to consider the
arrangements for the immediate future, choosing between the
majority view, which favoured a transitional two-year period in
which customers would continue to obtain their supplies and
services from HMSO, and the minority view, which supported
an immediate end to tying.

The Government opted for the safer course of fixing a date two
years ahead, 1 April 1982, and letting it be known that from then
on no Government Department would be obliged to use any of
the services of HMSO or buy any of its goods if it could obtain a
better deal elsewhere.

### A sea change

Though contemplated for so long, the decision to end the old
monopoly came as something of a shock to all ranks of HMSO
staff. However, the new Controller welcomed what he called 'this
sea change' as providing a more competitive environment in
which HMSO could prove its ability to provide value for money.
But what if a number of major Government customers ceased
trading with HMSO from 1 April 1982 'at a stroke'? Having just
completed the negotiations with the Treasury over the capital
structure of the Trading Fund, which left HMSO financially
handicapped by loans at very high rates of interest, the secession
en bloc of a third of its customers might be a crippling blow.
Would it not be prudent to have some kind of safety net to give
the organization a chance to prove itself, so that it was not

deprived overnight of the minimum turnover and profit sufficient to keep it going? To prevent the demise of HMSO for reasons which had nothing to do with its competitiveness or non-competitiveness – which it had not had a chance to demonstrate – the Treasury agreed that HMSO could negotiate Customer Agreements.

HMSO spent the two years leading to Untying Day approaching their Government Department customers one by one. It was of course entirely up to Departments whether they continued to buy from HMSO after they were no longer obliged to; but rather than make any precipitate decision one way or the other, would they sign an agreement with the Controller, which would not be legally binding, to maintain the status quo ante 1 April 1982 for a set period? In that way any market changes could take place in an orderly manner. As the Comptroller and Auditor General said in his report on the HMSO Trading Fund Accounts 1980–81:

> Proposals for untying have to be justified by comparative costing in accordance with agreed guidelines, having regard to the overall Exchequer interest and to public purchasing policy. HMSO are currently negotiating agreements with customer Departments on the provision of goods and services after 1 April. Under transitional arrangements operating in 1981–82 certain Departments were allowed to untie in limited areas of their business and all Departments were free to purchase commercially published books from commercial booksellers or from HMSO, whichever was the more economical arrangement . . . As regards 1982–83 HMSO informed me that it did not seem, as yet, that Departments were choosing to buy elsewhere on any significant scale except for HMSO reprographic services where turnover was expected to reduce by approximately £3 million compared with 1981–82.

By October 1981, six months before Untying Day, Sharp felt confident enough to state in one of his *Newsletters* to staff that 'the main potential threat to the future of HMSO . . . had been significantly diminished by the considerable progress which has been made with the negotiation of Agreements with nearly all Government Departments under which they have opted in almost all cases to continue to use HMSO goods and services, subject of course to review from time to time'.

Agreements with Government Departments who wanted HMSO's Publications Division to publish their non-Parliamentary books differed from those made with Supply and Print Procurement Divisions for the purchase of goods. These 'sponsors' were free to place their publishing elsewhere, but they too had to demonstrate overall Exchequer advantage. By the same token Publications Division, in accepting the publishing risk in the new commercial-style operation, were able to look more critically at the potential profitability of material offered.

## Making ends meet

Sharp told the Public Accounts Committee in July 1981 he had no doubt that the discipline of a Trading Fund, and the associated requirements for full costing and charging, had already had a beneficial effect on HMSO in terms of increased cost awareness. He saw the need to achieve specific financial targets as concentrating attention on reducing capital, reducing debtors, treating creditors more realistically, reducing work in progress and ensuring that large sums were not held up by inefficiencies in the accounting and computing processes. Moreover, to hit the targets they had to keep a tight control of the investment programme so that capital was invested only if it could earn a good financial return. Being financed by a Trading Fund, he wrote in *Management in Government*, had led to major changes:

> These have sometimes been unpalatable; no one likes seeing promotion opportunities diminish, colleagues retiring early or even made redundant. Yet, however unpalatable, clear-cut direction has been welcomed after years of uncertainty about the future . . . The structure of the organization has been changed from one where central functions predominated, with a cramping effect upon both the authority and speed of response, to a leaner, decentralized mode where people at the sharp end are directly accountable.

The effect appeared to be immediate, with a return on capital of 22 per cent being earned in the first year. The large surplus also reflected a larger volume of business than budgeted for. The good result had been achieved in spite of the fact that in that first year HMSO was 100 per cent debt-financed, and that on the Originating Debt of £50 million taken over on 1 April 1980, it had to pay an interest rate of 15¼ per cent per annum. Even the best of commercial firms, used to operating on an average 30 per cent debt ratio, would have had difficulty in servicing such a harsh imposition.

Because of the exceptionally good operating results for 1980–81, stated Sharp in a *Controller's Newsletter* early in 1982, meeting the interest burden was manageable. Moreover, in the current year (1981–82), when the surplus was expected to be much closer to the financial target, having to borrow to pay the interest was 'unfortunate but not a disaster'.

But costs had to be reduced further. The Management Group surveyed the list of properties occupied by HMSO and decided tighter control needed to be exercised to reduce resource costs. So Personnel Services Division undertook a systematic review of all HMSO accommodation and succeeded in cutting it to an even greater extent than the ten per cent which Management Group had stipulated. Establishments such as Atlantic House, Cornwall House, Wembley and Alperton, which had been synonymous with HMSO over very many years, were closed. Those members of staff who remained in London were mainly housed in the Publications Centre, while in Norwich the operating divisions were concentrated as far as possible in the new St Crispins building.


### Planning and control

Keeping HMSO on the course which each year led to it achieving both financial objectives was the role of Finance and Planning Division. Co-ordinating the budgets and forward plans of the four operating divisions was no easy task. When added to keeping the Department's capital investment under constant review, anticipating its need to borrow and keeping in touch with the Treasury, the Division's responsibilities were formidable. The professionals who now ran the Division were well versed in the techniques of determining capital requirements and financial priorities, the use of performance indicators, project appraisals and the rest.

The Division paid the contractors' bills of each of the four 'businesses' and accounted for the whole of HMSO's running expenses, including wages and salaries. They invoiced customers (with the exception of the non-Governmental customers for publications) for goods and services and collected the money due; and they prepared the Trading Fund's statutory annual accounts which followed standard commercial accounting practice as laid down in the 1981 Companies Act. For the staff and public there was an illustrated Review of the Year with abridged accounts. The full accounts were subject to audit on behalf of Parliament by the National Audit Office, who also carried out a continuous examination of the Department's transactions and systems throughout the year. The full accounts were published as a House of Commons Paper.

The key financial discipline for keeping HMSO moving in the direction of its targets was the April-to-March forecast of expenditure and income which each year formed the basis of a consistent but rolling Five Year Forward Plan.

The Forward Plan was the medium by which the Treasury was informed about the HMSO Trading Fund's operations. All the main assumptions had to be agreed with them. After approval by the Management Group, and with the consent of the Minister, the Forward Plan was submitted to the Treasury whose officials then discussed it with HMSO. Their agreement constituted approval in principle for the strategy and investment programmes outlined in the Plan and paved the way for final clearance by the Minister.

### The key to competitiveness

However sophisticated the systems and the electronics which made them work, none would serve its purpose without people – people moreover capable of fully comprehending their complexity and employing them in the most effective way. The Controller was at pains to declare his agreement with his predecessor that the Office's most valuable resource was its people. But he was only too aware also that offering keen prices depended to a very great extent on eliminating 'unnecessary posts'. HMSO would in any case have to make a substantial reduction in staff since the Government, as part of its retrenchment policy, was cutting the whole Civil Service to 630,000 by 1 April 1984. By a fortunate coincidence, the Controller told the Public Accounts Committee in June 1981, the aims of the Government and the aims of HMSO were perhaps not very far apart:

> The key to efficiency and competitiveness is manpower, because it is our main resource. Unless we are successful ourselves in reducing our manpower for commercial reasons, we will have a less secure future, and therefore our own aim as a commercial organization points us in the same direction as the Government are pointing us for different reasons.

Under the Vote system the emphasis had been on service with the cost of the service being secondary. Financed by a Trading Fund, HMSO still looked to service to retain its customers but had to ensure that the costs of that service were not more than its customers were prepared to pay. And that meant, among other things, reducing manpower numbers. To the considerable upheaval occasioned by the reorganization the trade unions brought a realistic approach. In spite of the 1980–81 result, it was more likely that from now on the volume of business would shrink. With the cutting down of the Civil Service there were going to be fewer repayment customers, and, with a lowering of their cash limits, less for them to repay. With the end of subsidies to Parliamentary publishing and with prices being charged to reflect their full cost, sales were expected to fall. In the context of having only enough staff to do the job asked of it, no more and no less, which was HMSO policy, it was likely that the work-force would be smaller.

### *'The worst is now over'*

Reducing staff did not mean that HMSO was skimping work or failing to seize opportunities for development. Aware that manpower savings tended to reduce promotion prospects to the detriment of able staff, a revised retirement policy for non-industrial staff, with an emphasis on retirement at age 60 rather than retention until age 65, was introduced with the agreement of the trade unions. By June 1982 staff had been reduced from more than 6,000 at the beginning of 1981 to just over 5,000. Within another 12 months the number had been reduced to 4,360, and the Controller, under the headline 'A Secure Future for HMSO', was able to tell his readers that 'the worst is now over'. They had just gone through 12 months of retrenchment and rationalization in which HMSO had shaped up to its new environment, and looked to a more competitive future. It was on course to reach its financial objectives for a third successive year. In the longer term the heavy investment being made in production units – for example £15 million on the new Publications Centre – would, with trade union co-operation, further improve profitability. The results up to the Bicentenary of 1986 fully justified this confidence. By 1984 staffing had been cut a further 16 per cent to 3,660 and reduced to below 3,500 in 1985.

Much of the strain of transforming HMSO into an Office not much more than half its pre-Trading Fund size was taken by the Personnel Services and Industrial Personnel Divisions, which were closely involved in assisting with management negotiations with the trade unions, calculating redundancy payments and dealing with staff surpluses. The trend was nonetheless towards greater line management authority. As the self-contained businesses they had been encouraged to become, each of the four businesses within HMSO took over greater responsibility for their own staff administration. Decentralization of this sort was advocated by the 1982 Cassels Review of Personnel Work in the Civil Service, which elaborated on the views expressed in the earlier Fulton Report on the merits of career development and the production of well-trained specialized staff with higher managerial and professional skills rather than the administrative all-rounder of the traditional British Civil Service. A more open style of personnel management developed, with even greater emphasis on equality of opportunity in recruitment and career development regardless of sex, marital status, ethnic origin or physical disabilities. An Equal Opportunities Officer was appointed in May 1984; and a Staff Involvement Committee with representatives of management and the non-industrial trade unions was established to discuss general issues affecting the way HMSO was run. As a result, communications between management and staff at all levels showed a marked improvement.

The drive towards making better use of people was assisted by the formation in 1983 of the new Computer Services Division which took over computing power and staff from CCTA who had run HMSO's systems for the previous decade. An effective in-house computing service which could be expanded for the major computer systems being planned was then available to the businesses of HMSO.

A sense of hierarchy had given way to common purpose, to job satisfaction, to professional pride at every level. Well-planned in-house training courses making full use of audio-visual aids and closed-circuit television helped the ambitious to qualify for promotion. Those who were ending their career could train for retirement. Machinery had long removed much of the drudgery of the clerical work of earlier days. And by the 1980s 'flexi-time' helped staff to fit their private lives more easily to work schedules.

CHAPTER 9

# Four businesses

## *Making it work*

What was the effect of the corporate theory at the sharp end? After all, HMSO was now completely dependent on successful trading: gross income had to be large enough to cover all costs, including salaries and pensions, and to put money aside to maintain the fabric of the business. And the only possible source for the money needed was the four risk-taking businesses of Supply, Print Procurement, Publications and Production. If even one of these failed, HMSO and its staff would be in deep trouble. It was therefore essential to ensure that all concerned had a very clear idea of where they were going in managing their businesses. As a first step, it was vital to analyse the worth of each of the businesses to HMSO as a whole and to adapt the plans for each to take account of the results of the study.

The potential risks were however alleviated by the fact that Supply and Print Procurement had proved themselves over the years to have a solid customer base which formed a reliable market. They were traditionally healthy businesses, with highly motivated and experienced staff who well understood their responsibilities and who easily adapted to the demands of management accounting and the new budgetary/monitoring systems. They could reasonably be expected to continue to provide an adequate net income which could sustain the organization while it tackled problem areas elsewhere. However, that was not to say that Supply and Print Procurement were not capable of making an even greater contribution. Although it was clear that the scope for further improvement in buying and trading techniques was limited, the fact remained that there was room for improvement in their resource management. In Supply it was also evident that the productivity of the warehousing activity could be significantly improved, while there was potential in Print Procurement for the introduction of new technology in the print-ordering process. So the Directors of both were given a clear remit to work out appropriate plans.

Publications Division was a different matter. The introduction of the Trading Fund regime had confirmed that it was a loss-making organization. Moreover, it was in a transitional period where its resource costs were distorted by new capital investment which was not yet giving a return. Nevertheless, as one of the largest publishing businesses in the country, with an annual out-put of over 8,000 titles and a traditional customer base, there was clear potential for viability and indeed a significant contribution to the overall HMSO surplus. Like Supply and Print Procure-ment, Publications also had the invaluable resource of a highly skilled staff which was fully committed to its work and generally held in high regard by customers. All agreed that its Achilles heel lay in the distribution of its publications, where the quality of service was poor and productivity far too low. The Director was instructed to work out a plan for moving more quickly to the new Publications Centre which was being built in Nine Elms Lane, near to Parliament and the Parliamentary Press.

Finally, the business analysis confirmed that the operational activities of Printing Works and Reprographics continued to be problem areas. The management of Works had been fighting valiantly over the years against difficult industrial relations arising from the general inflationary situation and the 'Fleet Street syndrome'. They were not selling their own products and services externally, but nevertheless their costs were reflected in the charges of the other three businesses and were therefore of vital importance to HMSO as a whole. Reprographics on the other hand did sell direct to customers. It was discovered that, on the turnover of about £10 million a year, Reprographics were making a loss of £2 million although employing about 15 per cent of the staff of HMSO. Part of the problem was that there was no direct clear chain of command for Reprographics – both the Directors-General had a responsibility for its operations. It was decided to simplify the structure and make each Reprographic unit directly responsible to the Director of the new Production Division which was formed by merging Reprographics with Printing Works. The Director was then told to develop a business plan concentrating on what Production was best at and on work for which it seemed there would continue to be a demand in the foreseeable future.

The four Directors now knew their future lay to a large extent in their own hands. Subject to their part in the corporate financial and manpower planning and control processes, they had a clear target to maintain, or in some cases achieve and maintain, viability, and thus ensure the long-term future of the part of the organization for which they had responsibility.

## Supply Division

Supply was large by any standards and by 1985 its turnover had risen to £150 million from £100 million in 1980. This had been achieved by building on the foundations previously laid, though not without some major changes.

The disbandment of the regional organization in 1981 gave the Division direct operational responsibility for the warehouses in London, Manchester and Bristol. These held the full range of items (paper, forms and office requisites) required to service all the customers in that region. Under a major reorganization in 1984 each became a specialized warehouse – paper in London, forms in Manchester, office requisites in Bristol – serving the whole of England and Wales. The two old warehouses in London, the over-large British Empire Exhibition Palace of Industry at Wembley and buildings at Alperton, were vacated and a new smaller warehouse leased at Park Royal. In addition, new buildings at Stakehill in Manchester were occupied to replace old wartime buildings at Heywood.

In March 1985 the London Garage was closed and responsibility for arranging its own transport in London was passed to each operating unit. Also in 1985 all contracting for England and Wales was centralized in Norwich. The former centre of its activities – London – was now reduced to the Office Machinery Technical Service headquarters and the Prestige and Conference Section, that small but important unit that provides the Royal Households and Parliament with a special service and helps meet the needs of international conferences hosted by the British Government. Virtually the only service still provided on a regional basis was that associated with the Representation of the People Act. That service still required the distribution of election materials to all constituencies at short notice.

The Laboratory was also re-organized. The Examiner of Paper of 1841 had expanded into a full laboratory service but, although most of its work related to Supply Division purchases, it had always been independent. In 1983 it became a part of that Division and in the autumn of that year moved to new premises in Sovereign House, Norwich, fitted out with the latest sophisticated apparatus.

On the actual supply side, office machinery presented the biggest challenge and greatest potential. The electronic revolution brought a surge in demand for more sophisticated typewriters: in 1980–81, 8,700 manual and electric typewriters were purchased; in 1984–85, 3,600 manual, 1,850 electric and 11,750 electronic machines. A total of 160 word processors were sold in 1980–81 and 1,400 in 1984–85. With its wide and detailed contacts throughout the industry, whether the need was for a hand-held calculator or specially designed equipment for a large unit such as that of the DHSS at Newcastle for whom it placed a £4 million order in 1985, Supply Division had the market knowledge, the technical back-up and the purchasing expertise to ensure that its customers got the best buy.

The regular servicing of these machines was carried out either by contract or by HMSO's own engineers when this was more economical. Although considerably smaller than in its heyday in the 1970s, the Office Machinery Technical Service still continued to provide a nationwide service and ensured that before any model of equipment was supplied to a customer it was tested for safety and quality.

42. HMSO's Norwich Headquarters; St Crispins (foreground) and Sovereign House (top left).

43. Training is a vital part of HMSO's support services. Closed-circuit television helps staff to see how others see them.

44. Computers provide the power to keep track of several million business transactions each year.

45. Management meets staff representatives at one of the regular Whitley Council discussions.

46. Control of HMSO's £300m turnover requires sophisticated financial planning systems.

47. Some of the wide range of office equipment and requisites provided by the Supply business.

48. Delegates at the 1985 Customer Conference in Norwich.

49. A lorry about to leave the new Park Royal Warehouse with paper for a printer.

50. The Office Machinery Technical Service offers repair and maintenance facilities.

51. Print Procurement covers the whole range of print from simple forms to high quality prestige products.

52. HMSO provides a design service using modern aids to increase accuracy and productivity.

53. Printing expertise ensures that quality in the design is maintained through to the final product.

54. New technology is now being harnessed to assist the print buyer.

55 and 56. The Publications Centre at Nine Elms (above) where HMSO stores and distributes nearly 50,000 titles using advanced computer-controlled warehousing systems (left).

57. The Publications business sells its titles internationally: a stand at the Frankfurt Book Fair.

58. The new Manchester Bookshop opened in 1985.

59. Hansard Press, where the verbatim account of House of Commons Debates is printed overnight for publication the next day.

60. The computer-typesetting control room at Hansard Press.

61. Taking the completed *Hansards* off the machine which has automatically gathered and stitched the sections.

62. Typesetting at the Macaulay Press.

63. George Thomas, Speaker of the House of Commons, with Barney Hayhoe, Minister of State, and William Sharp, HMSO Controller and Chief Executive, at the opening of Hansard Press in November 1981.

64. HMSO's Management Group, 1986.

## Print Procurement

As already indicated, Print Procurement was in the fortunate position of having a fairly steady business. Nevertheless, the Director needed to face the potential risks of the untying of customers. He decided to seek help from the Treasury in establishing that his performance indicators were sound and valid to a point where customers would be convinced that they were getting value for money. He was successful. The new indicators developed with Treasury help showed that Print Procurement was buying at about 25 per cent below the average bid prices they were receiving from the trade, and that the differential was growing.

A practical endorsement of these findings was made by the Ministry of Defence, Print Procurement's largest customer. The Ministry set up a temporary print-buying section of its own to seek prices direct from the printing trade in competition with HMSO. The experiment was intended to last a year, but was terminated after nine months when the Falklands war intervened, by which time it had established that HMSO prices were on average some 17 per cent below anything the Ministry could achieve for itself.

The two important factors which enabled HMSO Print Procurement to secure such prices were its unrivalled technical expertise and its comprehensive trade coverage – attributes which were later to be characterized in its 1985 marketing video as its 'know-how' and 'know-who'. The know-how derived, of course, from the practice of staffing the Division's operational functions with professional printers who had served their time as compositors, machine minders and the like, and then passed HMSO's own entrance examination to demonstrate their knowledge of print technicalities. The advantages of this professionalism are obvious: customers could be assured of expert advice on the most economical way of meeting their printing needs; and trade contractors could rely on having requirements spelled out in detail for them in their own technical language. This know-how was supplemented by the know-who. By 1985 Print Procurement was maintaining plant and staff records for over 3,000 printing firms throughout the length and breadth of the United Kingdom. They were classified according to size, quality and technical and product capability so that print buyers could home in on those best suited to producing any given job, and there were bound to be some in each group who would offer a good price in order to plug gaps in their production schedules. It is estimated that over 700 printers are doing work for HMSO at any given time.

By 1985 Print Procurement was doing more business than ever before, yet doing it more efficiently. Permanent staffing was being steadily reduced, and a sustained attack on the working capital tied up in the business was yielding significant results: careful housekeeping had reduced the stocks of paper held on printers' premises by about 50 per cent; new procedures leading to prompter billing of larger jobs had saved over £300,000 per annum in interest charges; and a reduction of £5 million had been achieved in the value of transactions locked up in the Division's complicated computer systems. But there was a limit to the improvements which could be made in systems first designed more than ten years previously. The plan was, instead, to replace them with a modern on-line database system known as Computer Assisted Print Ordering (CAPO). CAPO represented an investment of several million pounds for the central processing hardware, the specialist consultancy assistance needed to take full advantage of the latest technology, and the VDU terminals which would be in daily use on every print buyer's desk. The system would, however, pay for itself by reducing resource requirements and improving cash flow through the pre-estimating of job costs. This would have the valuable spin-off for customer Departments of improving the accuracy of commitment information available from HMSO – information essential for their monitoring of expenditure against cash limits. Fittingly, the new system will be brought on stream in this Bicentenary year.

### Publications

The main challenge the Director faced here, as already stated, was to improve the productivity and quality of his distribution facilities, and quickly. He set about this by simplifying the proposed new systems and getting into the new Centre at the earliest possible date, leaving refinements for later. This enabled the Publications Centre to begin operation for Parliamentary items at Easter 1983 with non-Parliamentary publications being brought on-stream during the following summer. By early 1984 all operations previously run from Cornwall House had been transferred to the Publications Centre. This had involved moving stocks of some 43,000 publications, and transferring details of 20,000 account holders and 80,000 subscriptions onto the new computer systems, whilst training staff in new procedures and continuing to receive some 1,000 orders a day. The result was that Publications and HMSO finally got the benefit of a huge capital investment of almost £15 million and at the same time shed the costs of operating out-dated facilities with poor productivity. In all, the central distribution staff were halved from about 500 to some 250. At the same time, the new investment significantly improved the turnround of orders and began giving customers not only quicker service but more reliable information.

The Director also made improvements in the operation of HMSO bookshops, only one of which (Cardiff) actually closed. He discerned that these bookshops were in the nature of regional centres and developed them in a way which increased their profitability.

The commercial-style operations under Trading Fund made it all the more important that the Division should be thoroughly professional in its approach to its tasks and the early 1980s saw a significant influx of talent and expertise from the outside world. Graphic Design had, of course, long been a specialist area and a centre of excellence. The Division also drew fully on the reservoir of expertise in other HMSO Divisions, particularly the technical knowledge in Print Procurement and Technical Services.

Qualified librarians were engaged to develop effective cataloguing to cope with the scale and diversity of HMSO's output. A bibliographic database was built and details of publications shown daily on Prestel. Direct ordering via Prestel and a regular microfiche publication covering all HMSO titles in print were introduced in 1985. The next step will be on-line access to the bibliographic database.

Sales and Publicity also benefited enormously from the recruitment of staff with relevant experience in commercial publishing houses. Agencies, both overseas and in the UK, were reviewed and trade arrangements improved. A computerized mailing list containing some 100,000 customers' addresses codified by subject interest and occupation was supplemented by bought-in mailing lists when necessary. In 1985 over one million publicity items were distributed, ranging from subject lists to leaflets promoting one or two specific titles. Press advertising, radio and TV broadcasts were arranged when appropriate.

The possibilities of alternative forms of publishing to the printed page were also explored. Microform publications became a regular feature and 'mixed media' packages of books and microfiche, or books and audio-cassettes and slides, were published. Publishing in alternative media was identified as a significant growth area and a strategy developed. As a result a 'Business Data Package' series was published. This is a highly innovative concept selling on floppy discs a compilation of statistics and information drawn from a number of sources, but all relevant to a particular industry, together with software to enable the information to be accessed and manipulated.

## Production

The Director decided on a twofold solution: rationalization of Presses and Reprographic units, with the shedding of activities for which HMSO could not see any long-term future. In essence, the plan provided for complete redevelopment with new technology of the two Parliamentary Presses in London, the high level Security Press in London and the commercial Security Press in Manchester. Telephone directory printing which utilized the largest portion of the staff was peripheral to the main purposes of HMSO and the impending privatization of British Telecom and their wish to assume control of the purchasing arrangements, especially of Yellow Pages, created the opportunity for HMSO to withdraw and thereby concentrate limited investment funds in crucial areas. It was decided to maintain the small general purpose Press at Edinburgh provided it was cost effective. As for Reprographics, the Director's assumption of direct command made the task of rationalization much simpler (and indeed led to a general perception that the regional structure of HMSO was an unnecessary luxury).

The decision on telephone directories was not taken lightly in view of the many years in which HMSO had printed these directories. The production was divided between the Presses at Gateshead and Harrow but the latter was grossly inefficient and compared most unfavourably with Gateshead. Harrow was therefore closed. On the other hand, HMSO was able to sell Gateshead as a going concern to a contractor who was ready to provide the large capital investment needed to modernize the factory and thus provide a long-term future for the staff still needed there.

The other main area of rationalization was the binderies. The view was taken here that the bindery facilities were dedicated to the needs of particular customers who should have the responsibility of accounting for their employment of the facilities needed to satisfy their requirements. The British Library Board and the National Library of Scotland therefore became the new employers of the staff, whose future was thereby made more secure.

Production, ably assisted by Technical Services, used the experience of computer-assisted typesetting gained with telephone directories to develop and install systems providing automatic page make-up for Commons *Hansard*; and it will also contribute to meeting the more complex requirements of Bills and Acts. Technical Services took the lead in advising customers on data capture from word processors for photo-typesetting with minimum operator intervention, giving HMSO Presses an edge in this developing area of work.

The difficulty of finding a suitable site for the new Hansard Press in London was finally solved by the Property Services Agency (PSA) using a developer who had a site, planning and finance for a leasehold building. The building was completed to time. With three other building projects foreseen to house the re-developing Presses, HMSO agreed with PSA that subsequent contracts would be managed by HMSO using PSA expertise on a consultancy basis. Subsequent buildings were completed to time and on budget.

In the first six years of the Trading Fund, the staff employed in the Presses and binderies reduced from 2,100 to 900. From the time of Production assuming management control of Reprographics the staff had reduced from 800 to 300. Throughout the period the production function met its financial targets on a year-on-year basis and, despite the extent of the industrial relations problems involved in these reductions, no significant industrial action was undertaken by any of the trade unions. Because of the increased productivity in the units which remain, increases in their prices have been below the general level of inflation.

The result of this activity has been to strengthen the position of HMSO in the printing area with its most important and influential customers. Parliament now has the benefit of a highly developed Parliamentary Liaison Office just across the road from the Palace of Westminster. It operates with hand-picked staff to the great satisfaction of most parliamentarians and officials of the House, including the Clerk of the House and the Editor of Debates. In the same way Treasury Ministers are most appreciative of the way in which the new security Press rises to every challenge with which they face it.

# CHAPTER 10

# HMSO today

*Overview*

As the Bicentenary approached, the four businesses of HMSO and their support services were therefore firmly structured to produce the saving to the Exchequer at which the Government aimed. By reducing the value of stocks from £28 million to £11 million, work in progress from £19 million to £13 million, debts from £79 million to £41 million, the resource-limited HMSO had successfully managed to reduce its capital requirements and so pay less of that crippling interest. HMSO had borrowed no more money since December 1981; all capital expenditure now came out of income.

It was an achievement which greatly impressed the Treasury, the guardian of financial integrity for all Government Departments including HMSO which, however, as the Controller and Chief Executive pointed out, was at arm's length from it. Nonetheless, for the free-standing HMSO which reported directly to the Minister of State, the confidence of the Treasury was essential. It was achieved. For in the spring of 1985 they agreed in principle to limit their financial control to approval of the HMSO Forward Plan.

'The very fact', wrote Bill Sharp in his *Controller's Newsletter* of 17 April 1985:

> that they feel able to accept this far-reaching departure from conventional practice is a measure of the confidence they undoubtedly have in our ability to manage our affairs effectively, and invariably achieve our financial objectives.

The success of HMSO's performance was illustrated in its
Annual Report and Accounts for 1984–85. For the fifth
successive year of its operation as a Government Trading Fund
HMSO met both its financial targets. There was a surplus after
interest of £4.9 million against the statutory requirement to break
even and the 12 per cent return earned on capital in current cost
accounting terms bettered the 5 per cent objective settled with
Treasury. Prices were held below inflation, service levels
remained high and there was a further 5 per cent saving in
manpower.

In his review for Parliament of the first five years of the
operation of HMSO as a Trading Fund the Comptroller and
Auditor General made a most favourable report, which led a
senior Treasury official to write that:

> You have every reason to be proud of your achievement. I have already
> drawn the Financial Secretary's attention to the C & AG's Report on
> your first five years as about the closest I have seen to a C & AG Report
> which makes no criticism at all.

In turn the Treasury Minister, who spoke in the House of
Commons debate on various Public Accounts Committee Reports, went out of his way to say:

> It is hardly to be expected that any organization, with the auditor's
> invaluable hindsight . . . performed perfectly in every respect, although
> the Comptroller and Auditor General's latest report on Her Majesty's
> Stationery Office Trading Fund comes about as close as it is possible to
> that.

But then of course Her Majesty's Stationery Office is not, and
has never been, a conventional Government Department but a
special organization geared to meeting the needs of a very special
group of customers. That is its purpose, where its skill lies and
where its marketing expertise is directed. Under the stimulus of
Trading Fund freedoms and commercial financial disciplines, the
four businesses and supporting corporate services, which in 1986
produced a turnover of nearly £300 million with a staff 40 per
cent smaller than in 1980, were making the fullest use of every
new technology which could be applied to their diverse activities

to help maintain and improve the service entrusted to Her Majesty's Stationery Office by Parliament over 200 years.

Edmund Burke and William Pitt could not but have approved of the way the successor to John Mayor's office in New Palace Yard is now being run. The fight against inflation may seem a less romantic incentive than the need to raise money for the fight against the rebellious colonists in North America, but it obviously motivated the dedicated group of men and women – non-industrial and industrial – who in the Department's Bicentenary year found, as so many of their predecessors had done, satisfaction and pride in making a successful job of being so special and trusted a servant of Government.

# Chronology

**1783**    On resignation of Shelburne (24 February), the Duke of Portland becomes nominal premier of a Charles James Fox/Lord North ministry in which Burke is Paymaster. As such Burke is responsible for seeing through Parliament the Receipt of the Exchequer Act which sweeps away many sinecure posts, including Usher of the Exchequer for which Horace Walpole holds the patent. The job included supplying the Treasury with paper, pens, ink, wax, tape and other items of stationery.

To implement (in part) the Receipt of the Exchequer Act, John Mayor of the Treasury is instructed to submit a plan for reforming the supply of Government stationery (25 July).

The Duke of Portland and the Lords of the Treasury approve Mayor's plan; on 13 December he makes an appointment to discuss it with Lord Cavendish on 19 December. But Portland's administration is replaced by one formed by William Pitt, and the meeting is cancelled.

Mayor writes a memorandum to the new Lords of the Treasury putting them in the picture regarding his plan (30 December).

**1784**    Parliament dissolved (24 March); Pitt wins general election with large majority and appoints Commission on Fees to report on extravagant charges being made (inter alia) for stationery.

With no reply to his memorandum of 30 December 1783 for 12 months, Mayor writes to the Clerk of Parliaments for guidance (20 December).

**1785**    The Treasury directs the Office of Works to prepare estimate for fitting up a Stationery Office in New Palace Yard (5 August).

Ann Grey (or Guy) hired as Stationery Office Housekeeper (10 October).

**1786**    **His Majesty's Stationery Office established as department within the Treasury with John Mayor as 'Superintendant' (5 April).**

First Report of the Commission on Fees (11 April), stating the expense of stationery was excessive.

**1787** Pitt chairs meeting at Treasury to review the new arrangement for supplying public office stationery (15 August).

**1788** Second Report of the Commission on Fees.

**1798** Lewis Wolfe takes over as 'Comptroller' of Stationery Office from Mayor.

**1800** Expiry of last patents.

**1802** George Dickins Comptroller.

William Cobbett publishes summaries of Lords and Commons debates as supplement to his *Political Register*.

**1804** In his *Parliamentary Debates* Cobbett publishes alleged verbatim reports of Commons speeches.

**1806** Treasury directs that Stationery Office should purchase paper, parchment and sealing wax by public contract.

**1807** New Stationery Office regulations; service extended to the ordering of printing. Cobbett has T.C. Hansard print his *Parliamentary Debates*.

**1810** Speaker of Commons sends printing bills for Stationery Office examination and advice.

**1812** Stationery Office moves from New Palace Yard to New Scotland Yard.

T.C. Hansard takes over publication of *Parliamentary Debates* from Cobbett.

**1820** George IV.

**1822** Select Committee on Printing and Stationery appointed; recommends a Treasury review of Stationery Office, which is undertaken by Alexander Spearman.

**1823** Spearman's Report recommends Vote Funding.

Alexander Spearman Comptroller.

**1824** Payment by each Government Department for its stationery and printing ceases; substitution of annual Vote from Parliament. First Vote £59,760.

John Church Comptroller.

Stationery Office divided into two: Comptroller in James Street, Storekeeper in Whitehall Place.

**1830** William IV.

Office of King's Stationer in Ireland abolished.

**1832**  Stationery Office opens branch in Dublin.

**1833**  Surrender to Stationery Office of office of the King's Stationer and Printer for Scotland.

**1834**  Fire destroys Palace of Westminster.

**1835**  Joseph Hume's Report on Parliamentary Papers (access to) which Commons accept; public can buy them at lowest price.

Select Committee on Printed Papers.

Vote for Parliamentary Printing united with Vote for General Stationery and Printing.

**1836**  Sale Office opened in Commons (run by Hansards).

**1837**  Queen Victoria.

**1838**  John McCulloch Comptroller.

**1840**  Parliamentary Papers Act giving Stationery Office staff protection from libel.

**1841**  Examiner of Paper appointed; Stationery Office buys paper subject to scientific tests.

Suppression of Printing Office for the Excise, Customs and Ordnance Services.

**1852**  Stationery Office to collect and sell waste paper from Government offices.

**1855**  Stationery Office buys 100 copies a year of unofficial *Hansard*.

**1856**  Two branches of Stationery Office re-joined; move to Storey's Gate (Princes Street).

Revised Stationery Office regulations; new form of agreement with printers.

**1860**  Treasury sanctions competition by invitation for Stationery Office printing and binding.

**1861**  Stationery Office takes over printing Admiralty Charts from Hydrographic Department.

**1864**  William Greg Comptroller.

**1874**  Stationery Office refuses to fine defaulting printers as recommended by Select Committee.

**1876** First request to Stationery Office for a typewriter (from Inland Revenue).

**1877** Sir Thomas Digby Pigott, CB, Controller.
Treasury recommends limited introduction of typewriters.
Reorganization of Stationery Office.

**1881** Digby Pigott's first report to the Treasury.

**1882** Sherbrooke Committee recommends Commons have all Parliamentary printing laid open to contract except *Votes and Proceedings*; Commons and Lords printers become agents of Stationery Office not Parliament; Stationery Office becomes a 'publisher'.

**1884** Fowler Committee Report praises work of Stationery Office.

**1885** Office of Works transfers sale of Ordnance Maps to Stationery Office.

**1887** Digby Pigott's second report to Treasury.

**1888** Lords Committee declares system of reporting debates inconvenient and unsatisfactory; Hansards' contract terminated.
Stationery Office becomes responsible for the *London Gazette*.

**1889** Queen Victoria appoints Controller as Printer to Her Majesty of all Acts of Parliament.

**1890** Digby Pigott's third report to the Treasury.

**1899** Free distribution of *Hansard* to MPs.

**1901** Edward VII.
Controller appointed Queen's Printer of Acts of Parliament in Scotland.

**1904** Digby Pigott's fourth report to the Treasury (written 1895).

**1905** Sir Rowland Bailey, CB, ISO, MVO, Controller.

**1906** Select Committee criticizes Ministries for publishing too much.
Scottish Stationery Office, Edinburgh.

**1907** Controller becomes printer and publisher of the *Votes and Proceedings* and *Journals* of the Commons.

**1908** Stationery Office distributes Old Age Pensions Act forms.

**1910** George V.
Stationery Office appoints first typewriter mechanic.

**1911**  Irish and Scottish agencies lapse.

**1912**  Mechanical addressing and warehousing equipment installed at premises in Shepherdess Walk, North London, to handle forms for National Insurance Act, 1911.

First Government sale office, Edinburgh (for two-year experiment).

Stationery Office Vote reaches £1 million.

**1913**  Sir Frederick Atterbury, KCB, Controller.

**1914**  Outbreak of Great War.

Stationery Office organizes printing of £1 and 10*s* paper Treasury notes.

**1915**  Sale of Government Papers throughout UK entrusted to Stationery Office.

**1916**  Northern Area Branch, Manchester; Forms Depot, Salford; Paper Depot, Oldham.

**1917**  Sale offices, Cardiff, Manchester, London (Kingsway & Abingdon Street).

Presses taken over in Hare Street and Bethnal Green.

**1918**  Press taken over at Harrow.

End of Great War.

Cornwall House completed as stationery and forms warehouse in Stamford St, South London, but requisitioned as military hospital.

Ulick Wintour, CB, CMG, Controller.

Stationery Office prints Lists and Registers of Electors for whole of UK.

Stationery Office takes over Foreign Office Press from Harrison & Sons.

**1919**  Sir William Codling, CB, CVO, CBE, Controller.

Stationery Office organizes reporting and printing service for British delegation to Versailles Peace Conference.

Stationery Office takes over India Office Press from Eyre & Spottiswoode.

Stationery Office takes possession of Cornwall House.

**1920**  Separate administration for N. Ireland.

Air Ministry weather reports printed by Stationery Office.

**1921**  Major reorganization: new appointments – Directors of Supplies, of Printing and Binding, of Publications, etc.

**1922**   Belfast Regional Office.

War Office Press taken over from Harrison & Sons.

Stationery Office starts producing telephone directories; publishing daily publication lists.

Type Faces Committee reports.

**1923**   Stationery Office assumes responsibility for Admiralty Chart Establishment production at Cricklewood (till 1929).

**1924**   Centenary of change to Vote Funding: celebration banquet in Connaught Rooms.

New representation of the Royal Arms.

**1925**   Paper Standardization Committee.

**1926**   General Strike: Stationery Office Presses affected; daily Government bulletin *British Gazette*.

**1927**   Gretton Committee Report validates principle of state-owned printing works.

Mechanical accounting system; units on decimal base.

Stationery Office takes over bindery at British Museum Library.

**1933**   First Clerks of Stationery Conference.

**1936**   Edward VIII.

George VI.

**1938**   Printing of 78 million ration books at Harrow Press begins.

India Office Press closes.

**1939**   Outbreak of Second World War.

Ministry of Information formed; Stationery Office subsequently produces best-selling booklets including *The Battle of Britain*, etc.

Western Area Branch, Bristol.

**1940**   Pocock Street Press destroyed in air raid; printing of *Hansard* moved to Drury Lane Press.

**1941**   Meteorological Office Press moves from Cornwall House to Dunstable.

**1942**   Sir Norman Scorgie, CVO, CBE, Controller.

Head office moves from Princes Street to Keysign House, Oxford Street.

Manchester Press (Chadderton) acquired.

**1944**  Presses of Vacher & Sons in Great Smith Street, and of J.B. Nichols & Son in Abbey Orchard Street, taken over.

**1945**  End of Second World War.

**1946**  MOI becomes Central Office of Information.

**1947**  Government sale office, Bristol.

**1948**  Contracts Division created.
Government sale office, Birmingham.

**1949**  Sir Gordon Welch, CBE, Controller.

**1950**  Co-ordinator of Reprographic Services appointed.
New warehouse, Sighthill, Edinburgh; Cardiff Regional Office.

**1951**  Head office moves from Keysign House to Atlantic House, Holborn.
Manor Farm Press.

**1952**  Queen Elizabeth II.

**1954**  Sir John Simpson, CB, Controller.

**1957**  Committee on Estimates hold to principle that Stationery Office exists primarily to serve Government Departments and not public and quasi-public organizations; Stationery Office Presses no longer limited to one third of the orders.
Xerography unit purchased; first Shepherdess Walk staff move to new Reprographic centre at Basildon.

**1958**  Computer at Atlantic House for administrative functions.

**1959**  Hutchinson Committee recommend more reprographic facilities in Government Departments.

**1960**  First Government Printers' Conference.

**1961**  Sir Percy Faulkner, KBE, CB, Controller.
St Stephen's Parliamentary Press opened on site of Pocock Street Press; War Office Press closes and its work transferred to St Stephen's, together with that of Abbey Orchard Street and Drury Lane Presses.
Meteorological Office Press moves to Bracknell.

**1963**  Duplicating and Addressing Unit moves from Shepherdess Walk to new building at Basildon New Town (officially opened March 1964).
Edinburgh Press acquired.

65. John McCulloch
Comptroller 1838–1864

66. William Greg
Comptroller 1864–1877

67. Sir Thomas Digby Pigott, CB
Controller 1877–1905

68. Sir Rowland Bailey, CB, ISO, MVO
Controller 1905–1913

69. Sir Frederick Atterbury, KCB
Controller 1913–1918

70. Ulick Wintour, CB, CMG
Controller 1918–1919

71. Sir William Codling, CB, CVO, CBE
Controller 1919–1942

72. Sir Norman Scorgie, CVO, CBE
Controller 1942–1949

73. Sir Gordon Welch, CBE
Controller 1949–1953

74. Sir John Simpson, CB
Controller 1954–1961

75. Sir Percy Faulkner, KBE, CB
Controller 1961–1967

76. Harry Pitchforth
Controller 1967–1969

77. Clifford Baylis, CB
Controller 1969–1974

78. Harold Glover, CB
Controller 1974–1977

79. Bernard Thimont, CB
Controller 1977–1980

80. William Sharp, CB
Controller and Chief Executive 1981–1986

**1964**    Decision to move to Norwich announced.

**1965**    Computer type-setting unit at Edinburgh Press.

**1966**    First volunteers start working at Norwich.
Technical Development (later Technical Services) Division.
Holborn Bookshop opened.

**1967**    Harry Pitchforth Controller.
First main move to Norwich.
Contracts Division disbanded.

**1968**    Main transfer to Norwich.
'Marks & Spencer Experiment' for purchasing.
Fulton Committee Report on Civil Service administration.
Acronym 'HMSO' becomes recognized usage for 'the Stationery Office'.

**1969**    Clifford Baylis, CB, Controller.
Gateshead Press opened. Computer-processed made-up pages.

**1970**    Industrial Relations Division formed.

**1971**    Management consultants propose better financial control systems for HMSO; Joint Civil Service Department/HMSO Review Team reports.
Introduction of decimalization.

**1972**    Lord Privy Seal takes over ministerial responsibility for HMSO.
Computer procurement transferred to Central Computer Agency.
Common Services Working Group examine principle of 'tying' Departments to HMSO, and HMSO's relationship with Parliament.
HMSO staff at 7,800.

**1973**    Government Trading Funds Act 1973.
HMSO included as a Department appropriate for functioning on basis of a Trading Fund.
Public Accounts Committee reviews progress on HMSO's new management accounting system.

**1974**    Harold Glover, CB, Controller.
Cessation of bookwork and general printing at Harrow Press.

**1977**    Bernard Thimont, CB, Controller.
Metric paper sizes; *Hansard* to be A4.

**1978**   New management accounting systems.

Further dispersal of London staff to Norwich; London Regional Office (Atlantic House); HMSO Laboratory remains at Cornwall House.

Harrow Confidential Press closed.

Full repayment system in Northern Ireland.

Industrial Personnel Division created.

**1979**   First commercial-style annual report; computer-based stock control.

**1980**   1979–80 last year of Vote Funding; HMSO Trading Fund Order.

From 1 April 1980 HMSO becomes a Trading Fund. Each customer pays HMSO for what it buys; but Vote Funding continues for Parliament.

Report of the Interdepartmental Working Group on Tying.

Harrow Security Press closed.

**1981**   William Sharp, CB, Controller and Chief Executive.

Hansard Press starts production, officially opened 17 November.

Manor Farm Press closed.

HMSO staff at 6,000 plus.

Supply and Print Procurement Divisions negotiate Customer Agreements; Publications Division, Publishing Agreements.

Reprographics brigaded with Printing Works Division to form Production Division.

**1982**   Government Departments 'untied' from HMSO from 1 April.

Harrow Press closed.

Manchester Press exclusively for security printing.

British Museum and Colindale Binderies transferred to British Library.

Edinburgh Bindery transferred to National Library of Scotland.

**1983**   End of HMSO telephone directory production with sale of Gateshead Press.

Publications Centre on stream.

HMSO Laboratory moves to Norwich (as part of Supply Division).

Belfast Reprographic Unit transferred to Government of Northern Ireland.

Computer and staff return to HMSO from CCTA.

**1984**   HMSO activity at Cornwall House ceases; all its operations undertaken at new Publications Centre with computerized stock control.

Metric paper sizes; A4 agreed for all Parliamentary Papers.

Business Data Packages Project (floppy disks).

**1985**   Development of major new computer systems, including Computer Assisted Print Ordering (CAPO).

All contracting by Supply Division transferred to Norwich.

Treasury extends delegation to HMSO of its financial authority. Now limited in principle to annual approval of HMSO Five Year Forward Plan.

Macaulay Press opened.

HMSO staff at 3,400.

**1986**   **Bicentenary of Her Majesty's Stationery Office.**

# Bibliography

BADENOCH, A. (1983) *OMRS in Edinburgh* (unpublished MS).

BARKER, W.R. (1925) Government Publications, *The Nineteenth Century and After*.

EARL OF BEACONSFIELD Speech in Lords on Digby Pigott's appointment as Controller, *Times*, 19 July 1877.

Biographical sketch of the late John Ramsay McCulloch Esq., with a list of his works, *Scotsman*, 15 November 1864.

BURKE, EDMUND (various dates) Letters to William Pitt 1783–1804. Public Record Office (PRO) 30/8, 102, 118.

CHAPMAN, E.H. (1973) *Ramblings of a Victorian Quill-Driver* (unpublished MS).

CHERNS, J.J. (1982) Her Majesty's Stationery Office, in *Yearbook of the Gutenberg University, 1982*.

CODLING, W.R. (1917) *Report to the Controller* (re visit to Army Printing and Stationery Depots in France, report dated 17 July 1917) (unpublished MS).

COLLINS, P. (1984) *Brief History of HMSO Belfast* (unpublished MS).

COMMITTEE OF THE CIVIL SERVICE (1968) *The Civil Service, Vol 1, Report of the Committee 1966–68* (Chairman Lord Fulton) (Cmnd 3638) (London: HMSO).

COX, WILLIAM (1961) *Crown Copyright* (HMSO).

COX, WILLIAM (1961) *Pricing Policy for Government Publications and Publishing Financial Statement* (HMSO).

COX, WILLIAM (1961) *Purchasing and Contracting 1786–1960* (HMSO).

COX, WILLIAM (1962) *Government Publishing and Bookselling* (HMSO).

DASHFIELD, D.C. (1955) History of HMSO, *Parliamentary Affairs*, 8(2).

DAVIES, A. (1984) *HMSO's Financial Management System* (unpublished MS).

DODSON, A. (undated) *Five Years' Typography: the HMSO Layout Section 1954–59* (unpublished MS).

DODSON, A. (1957) *Blue Books and Others*.

GREG, W.R. (1866) *Memorandum* (re pernicious practice of borrowing money, 2 August 1866) HMSO Archives.

GREG, W.R. (1866) *Memorandum* (re trust for porters' funerals, 16 May 1866). HMSO Archives.

GUILCHER, G. (undated) *Principaux Papiers sur la Preparation, la Publication, la Diffusion, et la Vente des Rapports Parlementaires Britanniques, 1817–1916* (Published as appendix to Guilcher, G. (1980) Guide des P.P. Britanniques, *La Revue Française de Civilisation Britannique*.

HANDOVER, PHYLLIS (1965) *A History of the London Gazette 1665–1965* (London: HMSO).

HMSO (1807) *Regulations for His Majesty's Stationery Office* 24 August 1807. HMSO Archives.

HMSO (1874) *Memorandum* (to HM Treasury, on General Measures of Economy) HMSO Archives.

HMSO (1887) *Confidential Memorandum* (from Digby Pigott to Cabinet re notice of motion, from Henry Labouchere MP, to reduce the Vote on Civil Service estimates by £2,000 in connection with the cost of *Hansard*).

HMSO (1877) *Confidential Report* (to HM Treasury recommending Central Printing Press, 30 July 1877) PRO T.I.168/6.

HMSO (1919) *HMSO: the Northern Area Branch: Synopsis of Two Years' Work 1916–1918* (Manchester: HMSO).

HMSO (various dates) Controllers' Private Letter Books:
Out, official 1864–1916 PRO Stat 6/2, 3, 4, 5;
Out, semi-official 1890–1947 PRO Stat 6/8, 9, 10, 11, 12;
In letters from HM Treasury
11 February 1798 – 10 July 1801 PRO Stat 1/1
   1802–42 PRO Stat 1/2, 3, 9, 10, 11, 12, 13
   1861–65 PRO Stat 2/2
   1872–74 PRO Stat 2/5
   1877    PRO Stat 2/8
   1905    PRO Stat 2/36
   1919    PRO Stat 2/50
   1942    PRO Stat 2/57

HMSO (1984) *Brief Chronology of Events in the Development of Computer Typesetting in HMSO* (unpublished MS).

HMSO (1984) *The History of HMSO Print Procurement* (unpublished MS).

HMSO (1984) *HMSO Finance Handbook* (unpublished MS).

HMSO (1984) *Personnel Services Division Since 1968* (unpublished MS).

HMSO (1984) *HMSO Production Division: History of the Presses* (unpublished MS).

HMSO (1984) *HMSO Publications Division: A Short History* (unpublished MS).

HMSO (1984) *HMSO Edinburgh: A Brief History 1906–1970* (unpublished MS).

HMSO (undated) *History of Forms Store and Distribution at HMSO Manchester 1908–64* (unpublished MS).

HMSO (undated) *HMSO Manchester Press 1967–75* (unpublished MS).

HMSO (undated) *Official Printing for the Coronation of 1953* (unpublished MS).

HM TREASURY (1787) *Treasury Minute* (15 August 1787, Establishment and Regulations for the Supply of Stationery) PRO T.I.29/58, copy S/N 398.

HM TREASURY (1823) *Treasury Minute* (21 March 1823, Stationery Office Establishment and Mode of Business). Transcript from copy in HMSO Archives.

HM TREASURY (1870) *Treasury Instruction* (26 January 1870, re Dispatch Boxes). HMSO Archives.

HM TREASURY (1884) *Treasury Minute* (29 March 1884, re Stationery and Printing Expenditure). HMSO Archives.

*House of Commons Official Report* Vol 981, 25 March 1980, cols 1377–1397 (Debate on HMSO Trading Fund).

KING-HALL, STEPHEN, and DEWAR, ANN (1952) *History in Hansard 1803–1900* (London: Constable).

LLOYD, C.G. (1984) *HMSO in 1936* (unpublished MS).

LLOYD, C.G. (1984) *HMSO Supply Division* (unpublished MS).

MAGNUS, PHILIP (1939) *Edmund Burke: A Life* (London: John Murray).

MAYOR, JOHN (1783) *Memorandum* (to HM Treasury, 30 December 1783, re Supplying the Various Offices with Stationery). PRO T.I.592/782.

MAYOR, JOHN (1784) *Memorandum* (to George Rose Esq, Clerk of the Parliaments, 20 December 1784, for his Appointment to Control the Reform of Abuses of Stationery). PRO T.I.601/808.

MAYOR, JOHN (1785) *Memorandum* (to HM Treasury, 13 August 1785). PRO T.I.623/1820.

MAYOR, JOHN (1786) *Inventory of Necessaries* (10 March 1786). PRO T.I.628/632.

MAYOR, JOHN (1786) *Memorandum* (to HM Treasury, 14 June 1786). PRO T.I.631/1440.

MAYOR, JOHN (1786) *Memorandum* (to HM Treasury, 30 June 1786). PRO T.I.632/1584.

MCCULLOCH, J. (1864) *Memorandum* (re Office Hours, 25 May 1864). HMSO Archives.

MCGRATH, P. (1958) *Government Publishing and Libraries* (Paper presented at the Annual Conference of the Library Association, Brighton). (unpublished MS).

MURRAY, THOMAS (1911) *Autobiographical Notes*, edited by John Fairley (Dumfries, Standard Office).

NAPHTHINE, DAVID (undated) *Harry Carter: Fragments of Memory, 1901–82* (unpublished MS).

OLLÉ, JAMES G. (1965) *An Introduction to British Government Publications* (London: Association of Assistant Librarians).

*The Poor Relation, The Times*, 1 May 1937.

*Profligate Expenditure, The Times*, 4 May 1861 (Leading article on expenditure by Government Departments on Stationery).

*Reduction of the National Expenditure, Standard*, 22 February 1873.

REID, H.G. (1881) On the Origin and Growth of the Stationery Office, Appendix A to *First Report of the Controller of the Stationery Office* (Command Paper C2782) (London: HMSO).

SCORGIE, N.G. (1931) *Memorandum* (on the Expenditure of HMSO, 10 April 1931, presented to the Committee on National Expenditure).

SMITH, A.A. (1984) *The Latest Developments in Print Procurement* (Paper presented to the Government Printers' Conference, 1984) (unpublished MS).

TREWIN, J.C., and KING, E.M. (1952) *Printer to the House: The Story of Hansard* (London: Methuen).
TURNER, G. (1984) *The New HMSO Publications Centre* (unpublished MS).
WALPOLE, HORACE (1780) *Memoir Relative to his Income* (London).

# Index

*Plate numbers are shown in italics*